50 Places to Visit Before You Die

A Traveller's Ultimate Bucket List

Steve Rogers

Table of Contents

Introduction

Creating a bucket list of places to visit allows us to dream, set goals, and experience the world in a way that goes beyond our everyday lives. It gives us something to look forward to, a sense of purpose, and a reason to step out of our comfort zones.

The world eagerly awaits our exploration of its treasures, and a bucket list is a perfect reminder that we should live life to the fullest. When we draw up a bucket list, we put our aspirations and desires first. It helps us focus on what truly matters to us and gives us motivation to work towards achieving those goals. By setting our sights on specific destinations, we are more likely to take action and make our travel dreams a reality.

When a person dies, it is usually said that they have kicked the bucket; therefore, a bucket list is the list of things that you intend to do before you kick the bucket. It represents a list of things we want to do or places we want to visit before we "kick the bucket." While the idea of a bucket list may seem morbid at first, it actually serves as a reminder to live life to the fullest and make the most of our time on Earth.

Having a bucket list provides several benefits. Firstly, it gives us a sense of purpose and direction. It helps us make decisions that align with our desires and passions and put our goals first. Secondly, it helps us embrace new experiences, thus pushing us out of our comfort zones. By striving to complete our bucket list, we challenge ourselves to try new things and grow as individuals.

Lastly, it creates lasting memories and stories to share. The experiences we have while checking items off our bucket list become part of our personal narrative, shaping who we are and how we see the world.

The book, *50 Places to Visit Before You Die* is your ultimate guide to the most awe-inspiring destinations around the world. It is designed to ignite your wanderlust, inspire your travel dreams, and provide you with practical tips and recommendations to make those dreams a reality.

This book has carefully curated a collection of 50 destinations that showcase the best of what the world has to offer. From iconic landmarks to hidden gems, from bustling cities to remote natural wonders, each destination has been chosen for its unique beauty, cultural significance, and transformative experiences.

This is not just a coffee table book or a source of inspiration; *50 Places to Visit Before You Die* is a practical guide that will help you plan your own travel adventures. By providing you with a list of must-visit destinations, it will help you create lasting memories that you can cherish for years to come.

Chapter 1:

Planning Your Journey

Creating Your Bucket List

Planning a trip and creating a bucket list can be an exciting and fulfilling experience. Whether you are a seasoned traveller or just starting out, having a well-thought-out plan can make all the difference in ensuring you have an amazing and memorable journey. Here are some tips and tricks to help you get started:

1. Research: The first step in planning your trip is to gather as much information as possible. Research your destination(s), including the best time to visit, must-see attractions, local customs, and any necessary travel documents.

2. Set a budget: Before you start making any bookings or reservations, it is important to determine your budget. Consider your accommodation, transportation, meals, activities, and any additional expenses like travel insurance. Having a clear understanding of your financial limitations will help you make

informed decisions throughout the planning process.

   A. Also, before you travel, take the time to familiarise yourself with the currency of the country you will be visiting. Know the exchange rate and keep in mind that rates can fluctuate, so it is a good idea to check again closer to your departure date.

   B. While most airports and popular tourist destinations have currency exchange booths, they often charge higher fees and offer less favourable rates. To get the best value for your money, consider exchanging a small amount of cash at the bank before you leave.

   C. If you plan on using your credit or debit card while travelling, let your bank know in advance. This will help avoid any potential issues with your card being blocked due to suspicious activity.

3. Immerse yourself in the local culture: One of the most rewarding aspects of travel is experiencing different cultures. Be respectful of local customs and traditions, try the local cuisine, learn basic phrases in the local language, and interact with locals to gain a deeper understanding of their way of life.

4. Stay connected: In today's digital age, staying connected while travelling is essential. Make sure to check if your mobile service provider

offers international roaming or consider purchasing a local SIM card upon arrival.

5. Pack smart: Check the climate of the place and make a list of all the clothing items you might need to survive the weather. Remember that being comfortable is very important in order to enjoy your stay. It is always advisable to pack light—you can always buy what you do not have or have forgotten once you have reached your destination.

6. Book your travel arrangements: With your itinerary in hand, it's time to start booking your travel arrangements. Look for deals on flights, accommodations, and transportation options that align with your budget. Utilise comparison websites and consider booking in advance to secure the best prices.

7. Plan your itinerary: Once you have your bucket list prioritised, it's time to plan your itinerary. Consider the duration of your trip and how much time you want to spend at each destination. Be mindful of travel times between locations and allow for some flexibility in case unexpected opportunities arise.

8. Prioritise your bucket list: Creating a bucket list is a fun way to ensure you don't miss out on any must-see or must-do experiences. Begin by brainstorming all the places you want to visit and activities you want to try. Then, prioritise them based on your personal interests and time

constraints. This will give you a clear roadmap for your trip.

Remember, planning a trip is just the beginning of an incredible adventure. Be open-minded, embrace new experiences, and allow yourself to be fully present in each moment.

Chapter 2:

Exploring Natural Wonders

Majestic Landscapes: Mountains, Valleys, and Canyons

Everest Base Camp, Nepal: Trekking Amidst the World's Highest Peaks

Trekking to Everest Base Camp is a dream for many adventurers, and for good reason. It offers an opportunity to stand at the foot of the world's highest peak, Mount Everest, and witness its awe-inspiring beauty up close. The trek is not only a physical challenge but also a spiritual journey that allows you to reconnect with nature and yourself.

The Everest Base Camp trek takes you through some of the most breathtaking landscapes on Earth. From the lush green valleys of the lower altitudes to the rugged terrain of the Khumbu Icefall, every step offers a new and awe-inspiring view. Along the way, you'll also have the chance to interact with the legendary Sherpa people, known for their mountaineering prowess and warm hospitality.

Choosing the right time to trek to Everest Base Camp is crucial to ensure favourable weather conditions and clear mountain views. The best time to go on the Everest Base Camp trek is during the pre-monsoon (spring) and post-monsoon (autumn) seasons.

During the pre-monsoon season (March to May), the weather is generally dry and stable, with mild temperatures and blooming rhododendron forests. This is also the peak climbing season for Mount Everest so that you may witness mountaineers preparing for their ascent.

The post-monsoon season (September to November) offers clear skies, cooler temperatures, and stunning views of the Himalayan peaks. The trails are less crowded during this time, making it a popular choice among trekkers.

Before embarking on the Everest Base Camp trek, you'll need to obtain certain permits and make logistical arrangements. Here's a breakdown of the necessary permits and logistics:

- **Sagarmatha National Park Permit**: To enter the Everest region, one must have a Sagarmatha National Park Permit. This permit can be acquired in Kathmandu or at the trekking route's Monjo checkpoint.

- **The Trekkers' Information Management System Card**, or TIMS Card Trekkers can be tracked, and their safety guaranteed with the TIMS Card, a hiking permit. It is available via the Trekking Agencies Association of Nepal (TAAN) or the Nepal Tourism Board.

- **Employing a guide and porter**: Although you can hike to Everest Base Camp on your own, having a guide and porter can make a big difference in your experience. While a porter can ease your weight and add to the enjoyment of the journey, a guide can guarantee your safety and offer insightful information about the local way of life.

The Everest Base Camp trek typically takes around 12-14 days, depending on your pace and acclimatization needs. Here's a detailed itinerary for the trek:

Day 1: Take a plane from Kathmandu to Lukla (2,800m) and hike to Phakding (2,652m)

Day 2: Hike from Phakding to Namche Bazaar (3,440m)

Day 3: Attunement Day in Namche Bazaar

Day 4: Hike from Namche Bazaar to Tengboche (3,860m)

Day 5: Hike from Tengboche to Dingboche (4,410m)

Day 6: Attunement Day in Dingboche

Day 7: Hike from Dingboche to Lobuche (4,910m)

Day 8: Hike from Lobuche to Gorak Shep (5,140m) and trek to Everest Base Camp (5,364m)

Day 9: Trek to Kala Patthar (5,545m) and hike back to Pheriche (4,240m)

Day 10: Hike from Pheriche to Namche Bazaar

Day 11: Hike from Namche Bazaar to Lukla

Day 12: Take a plane from Lukla to Kathmandu

Must-See attractions and highlights along the way

The Everest Base Camp trek is not just about reaching the base camp—it is also about the journey itself. Along the way, you will encounter several must-see attractions and highlights that make the trek even more memorable. Here are a few:

- **Namche Bazaar**: Known as the gateway to Everest, Namche Bazaar is a bustling Sherpa town with colourful markets, bakeries, and stunning mountain views. Take some time to explore the local culture and visit the Everest View Hotel for panoramic vistas.

- **Tengboche Monastery**: The monastery is the highest Buddhist monastery in the region. It is located at a 3.860m altitude. Tengboche monastery offers a spiritual and peaceful atmosphere, with a breathtaking view of Ama Dablam and Mount Everest.

- **Everest Base Camp**: The base camp is the hike's ultimate destination. It provides hikers with an exciting and unique opportunity to witness nature's splendour as they set on their journey to summit the world's highest peak.

The Everest Base Camp trek awaits you—be ready to be taken on a remarkable adventure amidst the world's highest peaks.

Grand Canyon, USA: Witnessing the Awe-Inspiring Vastness of the Canyon's Layers and Colours

The Grand Canyon is a natural masterpiece carved over millions of years by the Colorado River. Its sheer size, stretching for 277 miles and reaching depths of over a mile, is a testament to the power of nature. This magnificent formation is a living testament to the Earth's geological history, with layers of sedimentary rock revealing a captivating story that dates back as far as 2 billion years. Each layer represents a different era, showcasing the ever-changing landscape of our planet. From the ancient Vishnu Basement Rocks at the bottom to the Kaibab Limestone at the top, each layer holds clues about the forces that shaped the Grand Canyon. The geological history of the Grand Canyon is a fascinating tale of erosion, uplift, and the forces of nature at work.

Unique Features of the Grand Canyon

The Grand Canyon is renowned for its unique features that set it apart from any other natural wonder in the world. One of the most striking features is the canyon's incredible depth, reaching over a mile into the Earth's crust. This immense depth creates a sense of scale and grandeur that is unmatched. Another unique feature is the variety of rock formations found within the canyon. From the ancient, dark-coloured schist to the vibrant red sandstone, the Grand Canyon is a kaleidoscope of colours and textures. The canyon also boasts an impressive array of geological formations, including buttes, mesas, and spires, each contributing to the overall beauty and diversity of this natural wonder.

Exploring the South Rim

The South Rim of the Grand Canyon is the most popular and accessible part of the canyon, making it the place's most popular tourist attraction. This side of the canyon offers breathtaking panoramic views that stretch as far as the eye can see. As you walk along the rim, you will be treated to stunning vistas, with the canyon's layers and colours on full display. The South Rim is also home to numerous lookout points, such as Mather Point and Yavapai Point, offering different perspectives and photo opportunities. For those looking for a more immersive experience, there are several hiking trails that lead down into the canyon, allowing you to explore its depths up close and personal.

Hiking and Camping in the Grand Canyon

Hiking and camping in the Grand Canyon is a truly unforgettable experience. With over 750 miles of trails to choose from, there is something for hikers of all skill levels. The trails range from easy, paved paths along the rim to challenging, multi-day adventures that take you deep into the canyon's backcountry. Camping in the Grand Canyon provides a rare opportunity to be one with nature and enjoy the calming environment of the canyon at night. Whether you choose to camp at one of the designated campgrounds or opt for a more primitive camping experience, the Grand Canyon provides a magical backdrop for a night under the stars.

Wildlife and Vegetation in the Grand Canyon

The Grand Canyon is not only a geological wonder but also a thriving ecosystem teeming with life. The canyon is home to a diverse range of wildlife, including mule deer, elk, California condors, and bighorn sheep. Birdwatchers will delight in the opportunity to spot over 375 species of birds, making the canyon a haven for avian enthusiasts. The vegetation in the Grand Canyon is equally impressive, with a variety of plant communities adapting to the harsh desert environment. From the iconic ponderosa pines to the delicate wildflowers that bloom in the spring, the flora of the Grand Canyon adds to its overall beauty and biodiversity.

Helicopter Tours and Other Aerial Perspectives

For a truly unique perspective of the Grand Canyon, consider taking a helicopter tour. These tours allow you to soar above the canyon, providing a bird's-eye view of its vastness and beauty. From the air, you'll be able to appreciate the sheer scale of the canyon and gain a deeper appreciation for its geological formations. Another option for experiencing the Grand Canyon from above is taking a scenic flight in a small plane. These flights offer a more intimate experience, allowing you to see the canyon from different angles and capture stunning aerial photographs.

Nearby Attractions and Day Trips

While the Grand Canyon alone is worth a visit, there are also several nearby attractions and day trips that can enhance your experience. Just a short drive from the South Rim, you'll find the historic town of Williams, where you can embark on a nostalgic journey aboard the Grand Canyon Railway. The railway offers a scenic ride through the Arizona countryside, culminating in a visit to the Grand Canyon Village. If you're looking for more adventure, consider visiting the nearby Havasu Falls, a series of stunning waterfalls located within the Havasupai Indian Reservation. The falls can be reached by a challenging hike, but the reward is well worth the effort.

Pack your bags and be prepared to be amazed by the awe-inspiring adventure of a lifetime at the Grand Canyon in the USA.

Torres del Paine National Park, Chile: Hiking Through Breathtaking Granite Peaks, Glaciers, and Serene Lakes

Torres del Paine National Park, a haven of natural wonders situated in the heart of Chile, is a UNESCO World Biosphere Reserve paradise for hikers and nature enthusiasts. It offers breathtaking views of granite peaks, serene lakes, and awe-inspiring glaciers.

The National Park is renowned for its awe-inspiring landscapes, which are dominated by the towering spires of the Paine Massif. As you hike through the well-marked trails, you'll be surrounded by the rugged beauty of the mountains, leaving you in a state of awe. The park is a visual feast, where every turn presents a new marvel of nature.

One of the park's most iconic features is the Grey Glacier, a majestic ice giant that stretches across the turquoise waters of Lago Grey. As you stand on the shores of the lake, you'll witness icebergs floating peacefully, creating a mesmerizing spectacle. The glacier's icy blue hues and colossal size are sure to leave you breathless.

Another natural wonder that awaits you is the Salto Grande waterfall. Cascading down rocky cliffs, this magnificent waterfall feeds into the glistening Nordenskjold Lake. As you approach the waterfall, you will be captivated by the vibrant colours of the water, which contrast beautifully with the surrounding lush vegetation. It is a sight that will make you appreciate the power and beauty of nature.

Hiking Trails in Torres del Paine National Park

The network of well-maintained hiking trails that are found at Torres del Paine National Park makes provision for trekkers of all levels. Whether you are an occasional hiker or a beginner, the park has something for everyone.

The W Trek is undoubtedly the most famous trail in Torres del Paine. Spanning approximately 70 kilometres, this trail takes you on a journey through the park's most breathtaking landscapes. Starting at the park's administration centre, the trail leads you to the base of the iconic Torres del Paine peaks, offering unparallelled views of the surrounding valleys and lakes. Along the way, you'll also encounter stunning glaciers, vibrant forests, and crystal-clear rivers. This trail is a must-do for anyone seeking an unforgettable adventure.

If you are looking for a longer and more challenging hike, the O Circuit is the perfect choice. This trail encompasses the entire park, taking you on a thrilling 130-kilometer journey through some of the most remote and pristine areas of Torres del Paine. The O Circuit offers a unique opportunity to immerse yourself in nature as you traverse rugged mountain passes, cross icy rivers, and witness the ever-changing landscapes of the park. It's a truly epic adventure that will test your endurance and reward you with unparallelled beauty.

For those who prefer shorter hikes, there are plenty of day-trip options available in Torres del Paine. The Mirador Las Torres trail is a popular choice, offering a relatively short but steep hike to a viewpoint that overlooks the iconic Torres del Paine peaks. The

Mirador Cuernos trail is another fantastic option, taking you to a viewpoint that offers breathtaking views of the Cuernos del Paine, a set of distinct granite peaks. These shorter trails allow you to experience the park's beauty without committing to a multi-day trek.

Before embarking on any hike in Torres del Paine, it's essential to be prepared and equipped with the right gear. Let's explore the essential hiking gear you'll need for a safe and enjoyable adventure.

Essential Hiking Gear for Exploring Torres del Paine

When venturing into Torres del Paine National Park, it is crucial to have the right gear to ensure your safety and comfort. The park's rugged terrain and ever-changing weather conditions require hikers to be well-prepared. Here's a list of essential hiking gear you should consider packing for your adventure.

- **Sturdy Hiking Boots**: A good pair of hiking boots with ankle support is essential for navigating the park's uneven and rocky terrain. Look for boots that are waterproof and comfortable for long hikes.

- **Layers of Clothing**: Torres del Paine's weather can be unpredictable, with temperature fluctuations throughout the day. Layering your clothing allows you to adjust to changing conditions easily. Pack moisture-wicking base layers, lightweight insulating layers, and a waterproof jacket.

- **Backpack**: A durable and comfortable backpack is essential for carrying your gear during hikes. Choose a backpack with a capacity that suits the length of your hike, and ensure it has a hip belt for added support.

- **Navigation Tools**: While the trails in Torres del Paine are well-marked, it's always a good idea to carry a map, compass, or GPS device to ensure you stay on track.

- **Sun Protection**: The sun in Torres del Paine can be intense, so pack a broad-brimmed hat, sunglasses, and sunscreen to protect yourself from harmful UV rays.

- **Water and Snacks**: It's crucial to stay hydrated and fuelled during your hikes. Pack a reusable water bottle and high-energy snacks to keep your energy levels up.

- **First Aid Kit**: A basic first aid kit is essential for any outdoor adventure. Include essentials such as band-aids, antiseptic ointment, painkillers, and any personal medications you may need.

By packing these essential items, you will be well-prepared for your hiking adventure in Torres del Paine National Park. Remember to check the weather forecast before setting out, and always let someone know about your hiking plans for added safety.

Tips for Planning Your Trip to Torres del Paine

Planning a trip to Torres del Paine National Park requires careful consideration to ensure a smooth and enjoyable experience. Here are some essential tips to help you plan your visit to this remarkable destination:

- **Choose the Right Season**: Torres del Paine's weather varies significantly throughout the year. The summer months (December to February) offer the warmest weather, with longer daylight hours. However, this is also the peak tourist season, so expect larger crowds. Spring (September to November) and fall (March to May) offer more moderate temperatures and fewer tourists.

- **Consider Guided Tours**: If you're new to hiking or prefer a hassle-free experience, consider booking a guided tour. Experienced guides can provide valuable insights into the park's history, flora, and fauna, ensuring you make the most of your visit.

- **Follow Leave No Trace Principles**: Torres del Paine National Park is a fragile ecosystem, and it's crucial to minimise your impact on the environment. Follow the Leave No Trace principles, which include packing out all your trash, staying on designated trails, and respecting wildlife and vegetation.

Recommended Itineraries for Exploring Torres del Paine

Torres del Paine National Park offers a wealth of natural beauty to explore, and crafting the perfect itinerary will ensure you make the most of your time in this remarkable destination. Here are some recommended itineraries that cater to different preferences and time constraints.

- **Short Visit (2-3 days)**: If you're short on time, a condensed itinerary can still provide a taste of Torres del Paine's beauty. Start with the Mirador Las Torres hike, which offers breathtaking views of the iconic peaks. Follow this with a visit to the Grey Glacier and an exploration of the French Valley for a well-rounded experience.

- **Classic W Trek (4-5 days)**: The W Trek is a classic choice for those seeking a moderate hiking adventure. Begin at the park's administration centre and hike to the Base Torres lookout. From there, continue to the French Valley, stopping at the Italian Camp along the way. Finally, make your way to the Grey Glacier, where you can witness its majestic beauty up close. This itinerary allows you to experience the park's highlights in a relatively short time.

- **Full O Circuit (7-9 days)**: For a more immersive experience, the Full O Circuit is the ultimate adventure. This itinerary takes you on a complete loop of the park, allowing you to explore its most remote and pristine areas. Start at the administration centre and follow the W Trek until reaching the John Gardner Pass. From there, continue to the backside of the park, passing through serene valleys, ancient forests, and breathtaking glaciers. This itinerary is ideal for those seeking an extended and challenging hiking adventure.

Remember to plan your itinerary based on your fitness level, hiking experience, and time constraints. It is important to allow for ample rest and recovery between hikes to ensure an enjoyable experience.

Wildlife and Flora in Torres del Paine National Park

Torres del Paine National Park is not only a haven for stunning landscapes but also a sanctuary for a diverse array of wildlife and flora. As you explore the park, keep an eye out for some of its most iconic inhabitants.

The guanaco is one of the park's most common and recognizable animals. These camelid relatives of llamas and alpacas can be spotted grazing in the park's meadows and valleys. Keep your distance and observe them from afar to avoid disturbing their natural behaviour.

Torres del Paine is also home to an array of bird species, including the majestic Andean condor. With its impressive wingspan, the condor soars through the park's skies, offering a truly awe-inspiring sight. Keep your camera ready to capture the perfect shot of this magnificent bird in flight.

If you are lucky, you may even spot the elusive puma, the park's apex predator. These solitary and elusive cats roam the park's valleys and forests, making sightings rare but incredibly rewarding.

In addition to its captivating wildlife, Torres del Paine boasts a diverse range of flora. The park is home to vibrant wildflowers, ancient forests, and unique plant species adapted to the harsh Patagonian climate. Take the time to appreciate the park's botanical wonders as you hike through its breathtaking landscapes.

It is time to make those bookings and travel to Torres del Paine National Park, a destination that truly captivates the senses.

Pristine Beaches and Coastal Marvels

Whitehaven Beach, Australia: Exploring the Dazzling White Sands and Crystal-Clear Waters of the Whitsunday Island

With its dazzling pure silica sand, Whitehaven Beach is not only visually stunning but also a dream to walk on. The soft, fine grains feel like silk beneath your feet, creating a soothing sensation as you explore this natural wonder. The beach stretches over seven kilometres, providing ample space for sunbathing, swimming, and enjoying various water activities.

The unique feature of Whitehaven Beach lies in its composition. The sand is made up mostly of pure silica, making it incredibly fine and bright. This composition gives the sand its bright white colour, which remains cool to the touch even on the hottest days. The sand is so pure that it squeaks when you walk on it, adding to the magical experience of being on Whitehaven Beach.

However, the beauty of Whitehaven Beach does not end with its sands. The beach is surrounded by lush tropical rainforest, creating a stunning backdrop that adds to its allure. The combination of pristine sands, turquoise waters, and lush greenery make Whitehaven Beach a true paradise on Earth.

The History and Significance of the Whitsunday Island

Whitsunday Island, where Whitehaven Beach is located, has a rich history and cultural significance. The island is part of the Whitsunday Group of Islands, which is a collection of 74 islands off the coast of Queensland, Australia.

The traditional owners of the Whitsunday Islands are the Ngaro people, who have a deep connection to the land and sea. The Ngaro people have inhabited the islands for thousands of years and have a wealth of knowledge about the area's natural resources and cultural heritage.

In addition to its cultural significance, Whitsunday Island is also an important ecological site. The island is part of the Great Barrier Reef Marine Park, a UNESCO World Heritage site renowned for its biodiversity. The marine park is home to thousands of species of fish, coral, and other marine life, making it a haven for nature lovers and conservationists.

Arriving at Whitehaven Beach

Reaching Whitehaven Beach is an adventure in itself. Most visitors access the beach by boat, either through a tour or by chartering their own vessel. A variety of boat tours are available, ranging from day trips to multi-day excursions. These tours often include snorkelling or diving opportunities, allowing visitors to explore the underwater wonders surrounding the beach.

For those who prefer a more intimate experience, private charters are available. These charters allow you to tailor your itinerary and spend as much time as you want on Whitehaven Beach. It is a great option for couples, families, or groups of friends looking for a personalised and exclusive experience.

Another way to access Whitehaven Beach is by seaplane or helicopter. These aerial tours offer breathtaking views of the beach and the surrounding islands. It's a unique way to experience the beauty of Whitehaven Beach from a different perspective.

Exploring the Dazzling White Sands

One of the main attractions of Whitehaven Beach is its pristine white sands. The beach stretches over seven kilometres, providing ample space for leisurely walks and exploration. As you walk along the beach, you'll be mesmerised by the pure white sand that sparkles under the sun. The soft, fine grains feel like silk beneath your feet, creating a soothing sensation as you make your way along the shore.

If you are feeling adventurous, you can hike to the Hill Inlet lookout point. This vantage point offers panoramic views of Whitehaven Beach and the swirling patterns created by the tides. It is a sight that will leave you in awe of nature's beauty.

Snorkelling and Diving in the Crystal-Clear Waters

The beauty of Whitehaven Beach extends beneath the waves as well. The surrounding waters are home to a diverse marine life, making it an excellent spot for snorkelling and diving. Explore the vibrant coral reefs and swim alongside colourful fish, turtles, and even dolphins.

Snorkelling gear is readily available for rent, and there are designated snorkelling areas where you can safely explore the underwater world. If you're new to snorkelling, guided tours are available to ensure you have a memorable and safe experience.

For those who are certified divers, Whitehaven Beach offers a gateway to the Great Barrier Reef. You can witness the amazing coral formations and see larger marine species, such as rays and sharks. by going on day trips and multi-day liveaboard trips to the outer reef that are offered by dive operators.

Wildlife Encounters on the Whitsunday Island

The Whitsunday Island is not only home to stunning beaches but also a diverse range of wildlife. Keep an eye out for the island's resident wildlife, including wallabies, goannas, and a variety of bird species. The island's rainforest is teeming with life, and you may even spot some of the rare and elusive creatures that call this place home.

You may also have the opportunity to spot marine wildlife during your visit to Whitehaven Beach. Dolphins are often seen swimming in the surrounding waters, and if you're visiting during the migration season, you may even catch a glimpse of humpback whales as they make their way along the coast.

Whether you are seeking relaxation, adventure, or a chance to connect with nature, Whitehaven Beach offers it all.

Anse Source d'Argent, Seychelles: Admiring the Surreal Beauty of Granite Boulders and Turquoise Waters

Anse Source d'Argent is well-known for its rare geological formations, displaying giant granite boulders that were formed by elements over time. These house-sized big rocks are scattered all over the beach and they create a breathtaking landscape that cannot be found anywhere else in the world.

The granite boulders at Anse Source d'Argent are not only visually stunning but also hold a fascinating history. These boulders are remnants of ancient volcanic activity that happened years ago. Over time, erosion and weathering sculpted these rocks into their current surreal shapes.

Walking among these gigantic boulders is a surreal experience as if being transported to another realm. The smooth surfaces, intriguing crevices, and unique formations provide endless opportunities for exploration and photography. The magical allure of Anse Source d'Argent is created by the contrast between the turquoise waters that surround the granite. The crystal clear turquoise waters are what stands out about Anse Source d'Argent.

The turquoise colour of the water is a result of the reflection and refraction of sunlight on the sandy bottom and the absence of sediment. This produces a breathtaking visual impact that is energizing and comforting. The water's clarity makes for great visibility, which is ideal for those who enjoy diving and snorkelling.

The Mesmerizing Beaches of Anse Source d'Argent

Anse Source d'Argent boasts some of the most mesmerizing beaches in the world. With its powdery white sand, swaying palm trees, and dramatic granite boulders, this beach is a true tropical paradise.

The soft, fine sand is a delight to walk on, and its pristine condition is a testament to the efforts taken to preserve the natural beauty of Anse Source d'Argent. As you stroll along the shoreline, you'll be awe-struck by the contrast between the pure white sand and the vibrant turquoise waters.

The beach is divided into several small coves, each with its own charm and character. Some are secluded and offer a sense of privacy, while others are more popular and bustling with activity. Whether you prefer a quiet spot to relax or a lively atmosphere to socialise, Anse Source d'Argent has a beach for every mood.

The granite boulders that dot the beach create natural alcoves and provide shade from the tropical sun. You can find your own little nook to unwind, read a book, or simply soak up the beauty of your surroundings. The beaches of Anse Source d'Argent are a haven for sun-seekers and nature lovers alike.

Exploring the Diverse Marine Life Around Anse Source d'Argent

Anse Source d'Argent is not just a paradise for beach lovers but also a haven for marine life. The lagoon surrounding the beach is teeming with vibrant coral reefs and a diverse array of marine species, making it a snorkeler's and diver's dream come true.

When you dive into Anse Source d'Argent's glistening pure waters, you will discover a colourful and breathtaking world. Numerous fish species, such as butterflyfish, parrotfish, and clownfish, can be found in the coral reefs. You may also spot larger marine creatures such as sea turtles, rays, and even the occasional reef shark.

Snorkelling is a popular activity for visitors who want to explore the underwater beauty without the need for scuba gear. With just a mask and snorkel, you can witness the kaleidoscope of colours beneath the surface and get up close and personal with the marine inhabitants of Anse Source d'Argent.

For those seeking a more in-depth exploration, guided diving tours are available, catering to both beginners and experienced divers. These tours take you to the best dive sites around Anse Source d'Argent, where you can discover hidden caves, underwater canyons, and a plethora of marine life.

Activities and Attractions Near Anse Source d'Argent

While Anse Source d'Argent itself offers an abundance of natural beauty and recreational opportunities, there are also several activities and attractions in the surrounding area that are worth exploring.

One popular activity is hiking. The nearby island of La Digue is home to numerous hiking trails that wind through lush forests, offering panoramic views of the ocean and the surrounding islands. The trails vary in difficulty, catering to both casual walkers and experienced hikers.

If you are interested in learning about the local culture and history, a visit to the L'Union Estate is a must. This traditional plantation showcases the island's heritage, with guided tours providing insights into the production of vanilla, copra, and other crops. You can also witness the traditional art of coconut oil extraction and visit the estate's giant tortoise sanctuary.

For those seeking a bit of adrenaline, kayaking and paddleboarding are popular water sports in the area. Hire a kayak or paddleboard and take your time exploring the coast, stopping to explore remote beaches and hidden coves. These activities are ideal in Anse Source d'Argent's serene, clear waters since they let you work out while taking in the landscape.

If you are a nature enthusiast, a visit to the Veuve Nature Reserve is highly recommended. This protected area is home to the endangered Seychelles paradise flycatcher, also known as the "Veuve." Take a guided tour to learn about the conservation efforts and spot these beautiful birds in their natural habitat.

Best Time to Visit Anse Source d'Argent

The best time to visit Anse Source d'Argent is during the dry season, which spans from May to September. During this period, the weather is generally sunny and dry, with lower humidity levels and less chance of rain. The water visibility is also at its best, making it ideal for snorkelling and diving.

However, it is important to note that Anse Source d'Argent is a popular tourist destination, and the dry season tends to be the busiest. If you prefer a quieter experience, consider visiting during the shoulder seasons of April or October when the weather is still pleasant but the crowds are smaller.

The wet season, from November to February, brings occasional rainfall and higher humidity levels. While the weather may be less predictable during this time, it also offers the advantage of fewer tourists and lower accommodation rates. If you don't mind a bit of rain and are looking for a more budget-friendly trip, the wet season can still provide an enjoyable experience at Anse Source d'Argent.

Anse Source d'Argent is a destination that truly lives up to its reputation as a paradise on Earth. The unique blend of granite boulders, crystal-clear turquoise waters, and powdery white sand creates a surreal beauty that is unmatched anywhere else in the world. Paradise awaits, and it's calling your name.

Navagio Beach (Shipwreck Beach), Greece: Discovering a Secluded Beach With Crystal-Clear Waters and a Stranded Shipwreck

Navagio Beach, also known as Shipwreck Beach, is a hidden gem nestled along the coast of Greece. With its crystal-clear turquoise waters and a stranded shipwreck, this secluded paradise is the perfect destination for travellers seeking a unique and breathtaking beach experience.

Navagio Beach captivates visitors with its dramatic beauty and untouched natural wonders. The rusted remains of the freighter, named MV Panagiotis, add an intriguing element to the already awe-inspiring landscape. This shipwreck, marooned in 1980, has become an iconic symbol of Navagio Beach.

The History Behind the Shipwreck

Many theories surround the origins of the shipwreck, adding to its mysterious allure. Some believe that the ship was intentionally grounded to avoid capture, while others speculate that it was a victim of bad weather. Regardless of its origins, the shipwreck has become an iconic landmark and a symbol of Navagio Beach.

The rusted remains of the MV Panagiotis serve as a reminder of the power of nature and the fleeting nature of man-made structures. The juxtaposition of the decaying ship against the pristine beauty of the beach creates a striking contrast that attracts visitors from around the world.

Location and How to Get to Navagio Beach

Navagio Beach is located on the Greek island of Zakynthos, also known as Zante, in the Ionian Sea. Situated on the northwest coast of the island, it is only accessible by boat. The beach is tucked away in a secluded cove, surrounded by towering cliffs, making it a hidden paradise.

To reach Navagio Beach, you can take a boat tour from the nearby harbour of Porto Vromi or the popular tourist town of Zakynthos. These boat tours offer a scenic journey along the coast, allowing you to marvel at the island's rugged beauty before arriving at Navagio Beach.

Alternatively, if you prefer a more adventurous approach, you can opt for a kayak tour of Navagio Beach. Paddling through the crystal-clear waters, you'll have the opportunity to explore the coastline at your own pace and soak in the breathtaking views.

The Beauty of Navagio Beach: Crystal-Clear Waters and Stunning Cliffs

Navagio Beach is renowned for its crystal-clear turquoise waters that glisten under the Mediterranean sun. The calm and inviting sea is perfect for swimming, snorkelling, and even diving, allowing you to discover the vibrant underwater world teeming with marine life.

As you swim in the translucent waters, you'll be surrounded by the dramatic cliffs that enclose the beach. These towering limestone formations, often referred to as the Navagio cliffs, create a majestic backdrop and add to the beach's secluded and untouched atmosphere.

The cliffs are a haven for adrenaline junkies and rock climbing enthusiasts, offering challenging routes and breathtaking views. Scaling the cliffs provides a unique perspective of Navagio Beach, allowing you to appreciate its beauty from a different vantage point.

Activities and Attractions at Navagio Beach

Beyond the stunning scenery, Navagio Beach offers a range of activities and attractions to keep visitors entertained. One of the most popular activities is exploring the shipwreck itself. You can climb aboard the rusty remains of the MV Panagiotis, capturing the perfect Instagram-worthy shot or simply marvelling at its eerie presence.

For those seeking adventure, you can embark on a thrilling speedboat ride around the island, taking in the coastal cliffs and hidden caves. The boat tours often include stops at nearby secluded beaches, allowing you to discover other hidden gems in the area.

Best Time to Visit Navagio Beach

Navagio Beach is a year-round destination, but the best time to visit depends on your preferences. The summer months, from June to September, offer warm temperatures and the highest chance of clear skies. However, this is also the peak tourist season, and the beach can get crowded.

If you prefer a quieter and more peaceful experience, consider visiting in the shoulder seasons of spring (April to May) or autumn (October to November). During these times, the weather is still pleasant, and the beach is less crowded, allowing you to fully immerse yourself in the beauty of Navagio Beach.

Other Beaches and Attractions In Zakynthos, Greece

Zakynthos is not just home to Navagio Beach; it boasts a plethora of other stunning beaches and attractions that are worth exploring. Some of the notable beaches include Agios Nikolaos, Makris Gialos, and Gerakas, each offering its own unique beauty and charm.

Beyond the beaches, Zakynthos offers other attractions, such as the Blue Caves, where you can take a boat tour and witness the mesmerizing blue hues of the sea caves. The island is also home to the iconic Venetian Castle in Zakynthos Town, where you can immerse yourself in the island's rich history and architecture.

Navagio Beach is truly a slice of paradise that will leave you in awe of Greece's natural wonders. Plan your visit, and prepare to be captivated by the allure of the beach.

Chapter 3:

Embracing Cultural Gems

Iconic Historical Sites and Architectural Marvels

Machu Picchu, Peru: Exploring the Ancient Incan City in the Andes Mountains

Machu Picchu is Peru's ancient Incan city that is nestled in the breathtaking Andes Mountains. The UNESCO Heritage site attracts history enthusiasts and adventurers from around the world by displaying its awe-inspiring beauty and mystical history.

Perched at an elevation of almost 8,000 feet, Machu Picchu offers a unique blend of stunning landscapes, architectural marvels, and a captivating glimpse into the Incan civilisation. From the iconic Temple of the Sun to the enigmatic Intihuatana Stone, every corner of this 15th-century citadel tells a story waiting to be discovered.

Exploring the Ruins of Machu Picchu

As you step foot into Machu Picchu, you'll be transported back in time to an era of ancient grandeur. The city is divided into two main sections: the agricultural sector, consisting of terraces and farming areas, and the urban sector, featuring residential and ceremonial structures.

The agricultural terraces, known as the "Andenes," are a testament to the Incan's mastery of terraced farming. These terraces were ingeniously designed to prevent erosion and maximise agricultural productivity in the steep mountainous terrain.

Moving deeper into the urban sector, you will encounter a variety of structures that showcase the Incan's architectural prowess. The Intihuatana Stone, a carved granite rock believed to have served as a solar calendar, stands as a testament to the Incan's deep understanding of astronomy and their reverence for the sun.

While Machu Picchu is undoubtedly the crown jewel of the Andes Mountains, there are plenty of other attractions and activities to explore in the region. The Sacred Valley, with its picturesque landscapes and ancient Incan ruins, is a must-visit destination. Explore the vibrant Pisac Market, marvel at the massive Ollantaytambo fortress, or take a scenic train ride to the colourful town of Maras. For adventure seekers, the Rainbow Mountain trek offers a challenging but rewarding experience.

Discover the secrets of Machu Picchu, immerse yourself in the vibrant culture, and create memories that will last a lifetime. Machu Picchu awaits, ready to unveil its mysteries to those who are willing to explore.

Taj Mahal, India: Marvelling at the Exquisite Beauty of This UNESCO World Heritage Site

The Taj Mahal is not just a monument; it is a symbol of love and a masterpiece of architecture. The Taj Mahal is situated in Agra, Uttar Pradesh, and was constructed in the 17th century by Shah Jahan, the Mughal emperor. The structure was dedicated to his cherished wife, Mumtaz Mahal.

As you approach the Taj Mahal, its grandeur becomes apparent. The pure white marble structure stands tall against the blue sky, reflecting in the serene waters of the Yamuna River. The symmetrical design and intricate details are a testament to the architectural genius of the time.

Stepping inside, the main chamber houses the tombs of Mumtaz Mahal and Shah Jahan, adorned with delicate carvings and inlaid with precious stones. The play of light and shadow through the marble lattice screens adds an ethereal touch to the whole experience. But the beauty of the Taj Mahal does not end there. The surrounding gardens, known as the Charbagh, are meticulously laid out in a geometric pattern, adding to the overall grandeur of the monument.

Whether one simply appreciates beauty, is an architecture lover, or history enthusiast, the Taj Mahal will definitely captivate your mind. When planning your visit to the Taj Mahal, it is advisable to go early in the morning or late in the afternoon to avoid large crowds and enjoy the serene ambiance fully.

From its stunning architecture to its rich history, this UNESCO World Heritage Site has all the elements to mesmerise you. So, if you ever find yourself in India, make sure to include a trip to Agra and witness this exquisite beauty firsthand. The Taj Mahal is worth every moment spent marvelling at its grandeur!

Petra, Jordan: Discovering the Ancient City Carved Into Rose-Red Cliffs

Petra, Jordan, is a mesmerizing ancient city that has stood the test of time. Petra is a UNESCO World Heritage Site, a city nestled in the picturesque landscapes, and is one of today's Seven Wonders World.

Petra's history dates back to around 312 BCE, when it was the capital of the Nabatean Kingdom. The Nabateans were skilled traders who established an extensive network of caravan routes connecting Arabia, Egypt, and Syria. This strategic location made Petra a flourishing city, attracting merchants and travellers from all over the world.

The Significance of the Rose-Red Cliffs

One of the most striking features of Petra is its rose-red cliffs, which give the city its unique charm and allure. These cliffs are not only visually stunning but also have a rich historical significance. The sandstone from which the cliffs are carved is believed to have originated from the Triassic period, over 200 million years ago. The varying shades of red and pink create a mesmerizing contrast against the clear blue skies, making Petra a photographer's paradise.

The Treasury: Iconic Facade of Petra

The Treasury, also known as Al-Khazneh, is undoubtedly the most iconic and awe-inspiring structure in Petra. Carved into the cliffs, it stands over 40 meters tall and is adorned with intricate details and decorative elements. The Treasury is believed to have been the tomb of an important Nabatean king, but its exact purpose remains a mystery. As you stand in front of this magnificent structure, you can't help but marvel at the skill and craftsmanship of the ancient Nabateans.

The Monastery: A Hidden Gem in Petra

While the Treasury steals the spotlight, Petra has many other architectural wonders waiting to be discovered. One such gem is the Monastery, located high up in the mountains. To reach the Monastery, you will need to climb around 800 steps, but the effort is well worth it. The Monastery is even larger than the Treasury and offers breathtaking views of the surrounding landscape. As you explore its intricately carved facades and vast interior, you will be transported back in time, imagining the lives of those who once inhabited this ancient city.

Petra offers an unforgettable experience that will leave you in awe of the ingenuity and craftsmanship of the ancient world. So, prepare to be captivated by the magic of this otherworldly destination.

Vibrant Cities and Urban Landmarks

Paris, France: Soaking in the Romantic Ambiance and Iconic Landmarks Like the Eiffel Tower and Louvre Museum

When it comes to romance and elegance, few cities can rival the timeless allure of Paris, France. From the moment you step onto its enchanting streets, you'll be captivated by the city's romantic ambiance and cultural grandeur. Whether you're wandering hand in hand along the Seine River, savouring a croissant at a charming sidewalk café, or gazing up at the awe-inspiring Eiffel Tower, Paris offers a mesmerizing experience like no other.

The Romantic Ambiance of Paris

Paris is often referred to as the City of Love, and for good reason. The city exudes a romantic ambiance that is palpable as you walk through its streets.

The charming architecture, cobblestone streets, and beautifully manicured parks all contribute to the city's romantic atmosphere. One of the most romantic spots in Paris is the Montmartre neighbourhood, with its narrow, winding streets and stunning views of the city. It's the perfect place to take a leisurely stroll with your loved one and get lost in the city's charm.

Another romantic experience not to be missed is a cruise along the Seine River. As you glide along the water, you will pass by some of Paris' most iconic landmarks, such as Notre Dame Cathedral and the Louvre Museum. The gentle sway of the boat, the twinkling lights of the city, and the sound of the water lapping against the boat create a truly magical atmosphere.

Iconic Landmarks in Paris

Paris is home to some of the most iconic landmarks in the world. From the majestic Eiffel Tower to the historic Louvre Museum, these landmarks are not only visually stunning but also hold a significant place in history and culture.

- **The Eiffel Tower: A symbol of love and beauty**

No visit to Paris is complete without a visit to the Eiffel Tower. This iconic structure, standing at 324 meters tall, is a symbol of romance and beauty. Whether you choose to admire it from afar or ascend to one of its observation decks for a panoramic view of the city, the Eiffel Tower is sure to take your breath away. Many couples choose to visit the tower at sunset, when the sky is painted in hues of pink and orange, creating a truly romantic backdrop.

- **Exploring the Louvre Museum**

The Louvre Museum is not only one of the largest and most visited museums in the world, but it is also home to some of the most famous works of art. The museum's collection spans over 9,000 years of history and includes masterpieces such as the Mona Lisa, the Venus de Milo, and the Winged Victory of Samothrace. Exploring the Louvre is like taking a journey through time and immersing yourself in the world of art and culture.

- **Other must-visit landmarks in Paris**

While the Eiffel Tower and the Louvre Museum may be the most well-known landmarks in Paris, there are many other must-visit sites that should not be missed. The Notre Dame Cathedral, a magnificent example of Gothic architecture, is one such location. It is breathtaking to see with its elaborate features and tall spires. Situated at the western end of the Champs-Élysées, the Arc de Triomphe is another noteworthy monument. Those who fought and lost their lives for France during the French Revolution and Napoleonic Wars are honoured by this famous monument.

Paris is a city that captures the hearts of all who visit. From its romantic ambiance to its iconic landmarks, there is something truly magical about this city. Prepare to fall in love with the City of Love.

Tokyo, Japan: Experiencing the Fusion of Tradition and Modernity in a Bustling Metropolis

Tokyo is a city rich in history and tradition, with numerous attractions that showcase its cultural heritage. One such attraction is the iconic Senso-ji Temple, located in the historic Asakusa district. This historic Buddhist temple, which dates to the 7th century, is renowned for its striking architecture and lively atmosphere and is a symbol of Tokyo's past. A colossal crimson lamp adorning the imposing Kaminarimon Gate will greet you as soon as you step foot on the temple grounds. Then there is the Nakamise Shopping Street, lined with traditional shops selling souvenirs, snacks, and handicrafts. You can take a moment to visit the temple's main hall and offer a prayer for good fortune and prosperity.

Another must-visit destination for history enthusiasts is the Edo-Tokyo Museum, which provides a fascinating insight into the city's past. The museum showcases the history and culture of Tokyo from the Edo period to the present day through interactive exhibits and displays. Learn about the samurai warriors, traditional crafts, and the evolution of Tokyo's architecture. The museum also offers guided tours and special exhibitions, providing a deeper understanding of the city's heritage.

For a taste of old Tokyo, head to the Yanaka neighbourhood, known for its preserved traditional atmosphere. Take a leisurely stroll along the narrow streets lined with wooden houses, visit the local temples and shrines, and explore the quaint shops and cafes. Yanaka Cemetery is also worth a visit, with its peaceful atmosphere and beautiful cherry blossoms during the spring season.

Modern Attractions in Tokyo

While Tokyo is steeped in tradition, it is also a city at the forefront of technological innovation and modernity. Akihabara, also known as Electric Town, is the epicentre of Japanese pop culture and electronics. This vibrant district is a heaven for anime and manga lovers, with numerous shops selling merchandise, game centres, and themed cafes. Explore the multi-story electronics stores offering the latest gadgets and devices. Don't forget to visit the maid cafes, where waitresses dressed in maid costumes serve food and drinks with a touch of entertainment.

To experience the future of transportation, head to the Odaiba district, where you'll find the famous Odaiba Rainbow Bridge and the futuristic transport system known as the Yurikamome. Take a ride on the driverless monorail, which offers stunning views of Tokyo Bay and the city skyline. Odaiba is also home to numerous shopping malls, entertainment centres, and attractions such as the TeamLab Borderless digital art museum, where you can immerse yourself in interactive and mesmerizing art installations.

For a taste of modern Japanese architecture, visit the Tokyo Skytree, the tallest tower in Japan. Ascend to the observation deck and enjoy panoramic views of the cityscape, stretching as far as Mount Fuji on a clear day. Another architectural marvel is the Mori Building Digital Art Museum in Odaiba, which showcases immersive digital art exhibitions that blur the boundaries between the real and virtual worlds.

The Fusion of Tradition and Modernity in Tokyo's Architecture

One of the most striking aspects of Tokyo is the harmonious blend of traditional and modern architecture. The city's skyline is dominated by towering skyscrapers, such as the Tokyo Tower and the Tokyo Skytree, which symbolise its modernity and economic prowess. These architectural marvels offer breathtaking views of the city and serve as landmarks that guide visitors through the urban maze.

However, amidst the modern high-rises, you'll also find pockets of traditional architecture that provide a glimpse into Tokyo's rich history. The Meiji Shrine, dedicated to Emperor Meiji and Empress Shoken, is a prime example of traditional Japanese architecture. Surrounded by a tranquil forest, this shrine offers a peaceful retreat from the bustling city. Its main hall, constructed using cypress wood, is a sight to behold, blending seamlessly with the natural surroundings.

Another architectural gem is the Imperial Palace, the primary residence of the Emperor of Japan. While the palace itself is not open to the public, the surrounding gardens are a popular destination for locals and tourists alike. Explore the vast gardens featuring beautiful ponds, bridges, and meticulously maintained landscapes. The architecture of the palace buildings reflects a mix of traditional Japanese and Western influences, creating a unique fusion of styles.

Exploring Tokyo's Bustling Neighbourhoods

Tokyo is a city of diverse neighbourhoods, each with its own distinct character and charm. Shibuya is one such neighbourhood, famous for its iconic Shibuya Crossing, often dubbed as the busiest intersection in the world. Experience the rush of crossing the street alongside hundreds of people, surrounded by towering billboards and neon lights. Shibuya is also known for its trendy fashion boutiques, department stores, and vibrant nightlife scene.

For a taste of old-world charm, visit the historic district of Asakusa. Explore the narrow streets of Nakamise, lined with traditional shops selling souvenirs and street food. Make your way to the Senso-ji Temple, the oldest temple in Tokyo, and immerse yourself in its spiritual ambiance. Don't forget to take a boat ride along the Sumida River and enjoy the scenic views of the city.

Another neighbourhood worth exploring is Shinjuku, known for its towering skyscrapers, bustling streets, and vibrant entertainment district. Visit the Tokyo Metropolitan Government Building and take an elevator ride to the observation deck for panoramic views of the city. Shinjuku Gyoen National Garden is a serene oasis amidst the urban chaos, offering beautifully landscaped gardens and peaceful walking paths.

Traditional and Modern Cultural Events in Tokyo

Tokyo is a city that celebrates its culture and traditions through a variety of events and festivals. One such event is the annual Cherry Blossom Festival, known as Hanami, which takes place in late March to early April. During this time, parks and gardens across the city come alive with the vibrant colours of cherry blossoms. Join the locals in picnicking under the cherry trees and witness the beauty of this fleeting natural phenomenon.

For a taste of traditional Japanese performing arts, attend a Kabuki or Noh theatre performance. Kabuki is a traditional form of theatre known for its elaborate costumes, dramatic makeup, and stylised movements. Noh, on the other hand, is a traditional masked theatre that dates back to the 14th century, featuring poetic storytelling and haunting melodies.

Tokyo also embraces modern cultural events, such as the Tokyo International Film Festival and Tokyo Game Show. These events showcase the city's influence on the global entertainment industry and attract visitors from around the world. Immerse yourself in the world of cinema or gaming and experience the cutting-edge creations of Japanese and international artists.

Tokyo is a city that never fails to fascinate, enchant, and leave a lasting impression on all who visit. Visit the city today and discover this dynamic metropolis.

New York City, USA: Immersing Oneself in the Vibrant Culture, Diverse Neighbourhoods, and Iconic Sights

New York City is a cultural mecca, home to a diverse range of museums, galleries, and cultural institutions. Situated on the famous Fifth Avenue, the Metropolitan Museum of Art is home to a vast collection that spans several countries and thousands of years. With items ranging from modern masterpieces to antiques from ancient Egypt, this museum provides an insight into the diverse history of humanity.

The Museum of Modern Art (MoMA), which features cutting-edge modern art from all around the world, is another important cultural site that you should not miss. MoMA is a centre for creativity and innovation because of its dynamic exhibitions and provocative installations.

Apart from these globally recognized museums, New York City is renowned for its thriving street art scene. Neighbourhoods such as Bushwick in Brooklyn and the Lower East Side in Manhattan are adorned with colourful murals and graffiti, showcasing the creativity and expression of local artists.

The Diverse Neighbourhoods of New York City

One of the most captivating aspects of New York City is its diverse neighbourhoods, each with its own unique character and charm. From the bustling streets of Chinatown to the bohemian vibes of Greenwich Village, there's a neighbourhood to suit every taste and interest.

In Harlem, you can immerse yourself in the rich African American culture and history, with its soulful jazz clubs and iconic landmarks such as the Apollo Theatre. Meanwhile, the Upper East Side is known for its luxurious boutiques, upscale restaurants, and world-class museums.

For an experience of the city's immigrant heritage, head to Queens, which is home to a melting pot of cultures and cuisines. From Indian curry houses to authentic Greek tavernas, you can embark on a culinary journey around the world without ever leaving the borough.

Iconic Sights and Landmarks in New York City

No visit to New York City is complete without experiencing its iconic sights and landmarks. Times Square, with its dazzling billboards and bustling crowds, is the beating heart of the city. As you stroll through this vibrant square, you'll feel the energy and excitement that epitomise New York City.

Another must-see is the Statue of Liberty, a symbol of freedom and hope. Take a ferry ride to Liberty Island and marvel at this majestic statue, which has welcomed countless immigrants to the United States over the years.

Central Park, an oasis of green in the midst of the concrete jungle, is a beloved retreat for both locals and visitors. Take a leisurely walk through its winding paths, rent a rowboat on the lake, or simply relax on the grass and soak in the beauty of nature.

New York's Arts and Entertainment Scene

New York City's arts and entertainment scene is second to none. Broadway, located in the theatre District, is synonymous with world-class theatre productions. From timeless classics like *The Phantom of the Opera* to groundbreaking new shows like *Hamilton*, there's something for everyone on the Great White Way.

If you prefer a more intimate setting, Off-Broadway and Off-Off-Broadway theatres offer a wealth of innovative and experimental productions. These smaller venues showcase emerging talent and push the boundaries of traditional theatre.

In addition to theatre, New York City is also a hub for music and dance. From the iconic Carnegie Hall to the lively jazz clubs of the Village, you can immerse yourself in a variety of musical genres. And if you are a fan of dance, be sure to catch a performance by the renowned New York City Ballet or the Alvin Ailey American Dance Theatre.

Lose yourself in the fast-paced rhythm of New York City and discover why it truly is the epitome of a global melting pot.

Chapter 4:

Immersive Experiences in Wildlife and Nature

Wildlife Safaris and Nature Reserves

Serengeti National Park, Tanzania: Witnessing the Great Migration and Encountering Diverse Wildlife

The Serengeti National Park is a breathtaking haven of wildlife and natural beauty nestled in the heart of Tanzania. In this enchanting African wilderness, you can witness the awe-inspiring Great Migration and embark on unforgettable encounters with diverse and majestic wildlife.

The Great Migration: A Natural Wonder

The Great Migration is one of the most remarkable natural events on Earth. Every year, over two million wildebeest, gazelles, and zebras make the treacherous journey across the plains of the Serengeti, seeking fresh pastures and braving crocodile-infested rivers. It's a spectacle of extraordinary proportions, as herds stretch as far as the eye can see, creating an awe-inspiring natural phenomenon that will leave you breathless.

During the migration, the Serengeti becomes a stage for an epic struggle for survival. The sheer number of animals attracts an array of predators, including lions, cheetahs, and hyenas. Witnessing a lioness hunting down a wildebeest or a cheetah sprinting after its prey is an experience that will stay with you forever. In addition to demonstrating the versatility and tenacity of these creatures, the Great Migration serves as a sobering reminder of the marvels of the natural world.

Best Time to Visit Serengeti National Park

The best time to visit Serengeti National Park largely depends on what you wish to experience. If witnessing the Great Migration is your top priority, plan your visit between December and July. During this period, the herds are on the move, crossing the vast plains and braving the Mara River. Witnessing the river crossings, where thousands of animals plunge into the crocodile-infested waters, is a sight you won't soon forget.

For those who prefer a quieter experience, the months of May to October offer a more serene atmosphere. The vegetation is lush, and the wildlife is abundant. It's also the dry season, making it easier to navigate the park and spot animals gathering around watering holes. Keep in mind that the park can get crowded during peak season, so booking well in advance is recommended.

How to Get To Serengeti National Park

Travelling to the Serengeti National Park is a journey unto itself. There are various routes to travel to the park, which is situated in Tanzania's north. The most popular option is to arrive by plane at Dar es Salaam's Julius Nyerere International Airport or Kilimanjaro International Airport, then take a domestic flight to one of the park's airstrips.

If you prefer a more scenic journey, you can also opt for a road trip. The drive from Arusha, a popular starting point for safaris, takes approximately eight hours. Along the way, you will pass through picturesque landscapes and have the opportunity to stop at other attractions, such as the Ngorongoro Conservation Area.

From the awe-inspiring river crossings to the majestic lions, every moment in the Serengeti is filled with wonder and excitement. The vast landscapes, abundant wildlife, and warm hospitality of the Tanzanian people make for an unforgettable experience. Serengeti National Park awaits, ready to captivate your senses and leave you with memories that will last a lifetime.

Galápagos Islands, Ecuador: Exploring This Unique Archipelago With Endemic Species and Stunning Landscapes

The Galápagos Islands are an archipelago bursting with breathtaking landscapes and teeming with unique, endemic species. Nestled off the coast of Ecuador, this pristine paradise is a nature lover's dream, where you can encounter some of the most incredible wildlife in the world.

Explore the islands at your leisure, witnessing the majestic giant tortoises that have roamed these lands for centuries. Dive into the crystal-clear waters and swim alongside playful sea lions, marine iguanas, and fascinating Galápagos penguins. Embark on thrilling hikes, surrounded by stunning volcanic landscapes and beautiful endemic flora.

The Galápagos Islands are not just a travel destination; they offer a once-in-a-lifetime experience. Discover the natural wonders that inspired Charles Darwin's theory of evolution as you observe the unique adaptations and behaviours of these captivating species.

Famous Wildlife Species Found in the Galápagos Islands

In addition to the Galápagos giant tortoise, marine iguanas, and blue-footed booby, the islands are teeming with other unique and fascinating wildlife species. One unique species is the penguin species found only in the north of the equator—the Galápagos penguin. These playful and charismatic birds are a joy to observe as they zip through the water with remarkable agility.

Another iconic resident of the Galápagos Islands is the Galápagos sea lion. These social creatures can be found lounging on sandy beaches or frolicking in the water. Visitors have the opportunity to swim and snorkel with these friendly creatures, providing an up-close and personal encounter that will leave you with memories to cherish.

The varied aquatic life of the islands is another well-known feature. Divers and snorkelling lovers have an opportunity to explore colourful coral reefs, which are home to the elusive hammerhead shark, the dazzling fish, and the graceful rays. Exploring the underwater world of the Galápagos is like diving into a living aquarium, with every dive offering new and exciting encounters.

Exploring the Volcanic Landscapes of the Galápagos Islands

The Galápagos Islands were formed through volcanic activity, and their landscapes bear witness to this tumultuous geological history. Exploring the volcanic landscapes is a fascinating journey back in time and an opportunity to appreciate the immense power of nature.

One of the most striking volcanic formations in the Galápagos Islands is Pinnacle Rock on Bartolomé Island. This iconic landmark is a result of volcanic eruptions and erosion, and its distinctive shape has become a symbol of the islands. Reaching the summit of the landmark provides breathtaking photo opportunities along with expansive views of the nearby islands.

Another volcanic wonder worth exploring is Sullivan Bay on Santiago Island. This otherworldly landscape is made up of vast fields of solidified lava, creating a surreal and desolate atmosphere. Walking along the hardened lava trails, you can observe the intricate patterns and formations that have been shaped by centuries of volcanic activity.

The volcanic landscapes of the Galápagos Islands provide a stark contrast to the lush vegetation found in the highlands. On Santa Cruz Island, visitors can journey into the misty cloud forests and encounter a completely different ecosystem. The highlands are home to a variety of endemic plant species, including the iconic Scalesia trees, which resemble miniature palm trees and provide a habitat for numerous bird species.

Immerse yourself in the captivating beauty of the Galápagos Islands, and let the unique flora and fauna leave an indelible mark on your soul. Discover a world where every day offers unparallelled discoveries and unforgettable memories. The Galápagos Islands await, ready to enchant and inspire you like no other place on Earth.

Ranthambore National Park, India: Tracking Tigers and Experiencing the Rich Biodiversity of India's Wilderness

Amidst the rugged terrain of Rajasthan, Ranthambore National Park stands tall as a testament to India's unwavering commitment to conservation. Here, amidst a backdrop of ancient ruins, you'll embark on a thrilling quest to track one of the world's most elusive creatures—the majestic Bengal tiger.

Ranthambore National Park is home to a remarkable variety of flora and fauna. The park's diverse habitats, including dry deciduous forests, open grasslands, and pristine lakes, provide a haven for numerous species. From magnificent tigers and leopards to sloth bears and crocodiles, the park boasts an impressive range of wildlife.

The park's rich biodiversity is a result of its unique location. Situated at the junction of the Aravalli and Vindhya hill ranges, Ranthambore National Park benefits from a mix of ecosystems. This convergence of geographical features creates a perfect habitat for a wide range of species, making it a paradise for nature enthusiasts and wildlife photographers.

Tiger Tracking in Ranthambore National Park

Embarking on a tiger safari in Ranthambore National Park is an experience like no other. With trained guides and expert naturalists by your side, you'll set out on thrilling game drives in specially equipped vehicles. The excitement builds as you traverse the diverse landscapes, keeping a keen eye out for any signs of the elusive tigers.

Tracking tigers requires patience and a bit of luck, but the reward is truly extraordinary. As you venture deep into the untamed wilderness, the air thick with anticipation, you'll find yourself captivated by the beauty of nature. The haunting calls of peacocks, the rustling of leaves as a leopard prowls by, and the serene glistening of lakes, reflecting the vibrant greens—every moment in Ranthambore is filled with wonder.

Ranthambore National Park Wildlife Species

While tigers may be the star attraction of Ranthambore National Park, the park is home to a diverse array of wildlife. The Indian leopard, with its elusive nature and stunning coat, is another prized sighting in the park. Keep your eyes peeled for the distinctive rosette patterns as you explore the park's dense forests.

Sloth bears, with their shaggy black coats and distinctive white V-shaped markings, are a common sight in Ranthambore. These playful creatures can often be spotted foraging for food or cooling off in the park's water bodies.

Ranthambore is also a bird lover's paradise, with over 270 species of birds recorded within its boundaries. From colourful kingfishers and majestic eagles to the vibrant plumage of the Indian roller, birdwatchers are in for a treat.

Best Time to Visit Ranthambore National Park

The best time to visit Ranthambore National Park is during the dry season, which extends from October to April. During this period, the vegetation is sparse, making it easier to spot wildlife. The moderate temperatures also make it more comfortable to explore the park.

It is important to note that the park remains closed during the monsoon season, from July to September, as heavy rainfall can make the terrain inaccessible and disrupt wildlife activities.

To maximise your chances of tiger sightings, consider visiting the park in the early morning or late afternoon when the animals are most active. The park authorities regulate the number of vehicles allowed inside the park, ensuring a more intimate and less crowded experience for visitors.

The untamed wilderness at Ranthambore National Park awaits, ready to captivate and inspire you at every turn.

Diving Into Marine Life: Coral Reefs and Underwater Paradises

Great Barrier Reef, Australia: Diving or Snorkelling Among the World's Most Extensive Coral Reef System

The pride and joy of Australia is the Great Barrier Reef. This 2,300-kilometer-long, internationally recognised coral reef system is a snorkeler's, and diver's dream come true. It is understandable why the Great Barrier Reef is recognised as a UNESCO World Heritage site, given the wealth of colourful marine life and beautiful coral structures.

The Great Barrier Reef holds immense importance and significance, not just for Australia but for the entire world. Various marine life, including multitudes of fish species and hundreds of coral, are inhabitants of this natural wonder. It plays a crucial role in maintaining the ecological balance of the oceans and acts as a nursery for numerous species.

Diving vs. Snorkelling: Which Is the Best Way to Experience the Great Barrier Reef?

When it comes to exploring the Great Barrier Reef, both diving and snorkelling offer unique experiences. The choice between the two depends on your comfort level and the level of immersion you seek.

Diving allows you to venture deeper into the underwater realm, providing an up-close encounter with the reef's vibrant marine life. With the guidance of experienced instructors, you can explore intricate coral formations, swim alongside sea turtles, and witness the majesty of manta rays gliding through the water. Diving also opens up opportunities for underwater photography and capturing stunning moments.

On the other hand, snorkelling offers a more accessible option for those who prefer to stay closer to the surface. Equipped with a mask, snorkel, and fins, you can effortlessly glide over the reef, observing the colourful fish and coral from above. Snorkelling is a great choice for families and beginners, as it requires minimal training and equipment.

Best Diving Spots in the Great Barrier Reef

The Great Barrier Reef boasts an array of exceptional diving spots, each offering its unique charm and marine diversity. Here are some of the best diving locations to explore:

1. **Cod Hole:** Located in the northern part of the reef, Cod Hole is famous for its massive potato cods that gather around divers, making for an incredible interaction. The clear waters and abundant marine life make this spot a must-visit for diving enthusiasts.

2. **Ribbon Reefs:** Stretching along the outer edge of the reef, the Ribbon Reefs are known for their stunning coral formations and abundant fish life. Divers can explore vibrant bommies and swim-throughs and encounter species like reef sharks, turtles, and giant clams.

3. **Osprey Reef:** Situated in the Coral Sea, Osprey Reef offers a unique diving experience with its sheer walls, drop-offs, and channels. This remote location is home to an abundance of pelagic species, including sharks, barracudas, and manta rays.

4. **Yongala Wreck:** The Yongala Wreck is a fascinating dive site off the coast of Queensland. This well-preserved shipwreck is teeming with marine life, including giant groupers, sea snakes, and schools of colourful fish. It's a haven for underwater photographers.

5. **Lizard Island:** Lizard Island is not only a tropical paradise but also a gateway to some exceptional dive sites. With sites like the Cod Hole and the famous 'Pixie Pinnacle,' divers can explore an underwater wonderland filled with corals, tropical fish, and turtles.

Best Snorkelling Spots in the Great Barrier Reef

If snorkelling is more your style, there are plenty of breathtaking spots in the Great Barrier Reef that cater to your preferences. Here are some of the best snorkelling locations:

1. **Green Island:** Located just off the coast of Cairns, Green Island offers an idyllic snorkelling experience. The shallow waters near the island are teeming with colourful fish, and the coral gardens are a sight to behold. Take a leisurely stroll from the beach and dive right into the underwater wonderland.

2. **Low Isles:** Situated near the town of Port Douglas, Low Isles is a popular snorkelling destination. The calm lagoon provides an ideal environment for snorkelers to explore the coral gardens, encounter turtles, and spot an array of marine life.

3. **Agincourt Reef:** As part of the renowned Ribbon Reefs, Agincourt Reef offers excellent snorkelling opportunities. With crystal-clear waters and vibrant coral formations, you can snorkel alongside tropical fish, turtles, and even reef sharks.

4. **Michaelmas Cay:** This small sand island is a haven for birdwatchers and snorkelers alike. After marvelling at the seabirds, slip into the water and discover the underwater world beneath. The shallow reef is home to an abundance of marine life, making it perfect for snorkelling enthusiasts.

5. **Heron Island:** Located at the southern end of the reef, Heron Island offers fantastic snorkelling experiences right off its shores. Swim among coral bommies encounter

colourful reef fish, and, if you're lucky, spot turtles nesting or hatching on the beach.

The Great Barrier Reef is a natural wonder that should be on every traveller's bucket list. Its unparallelled beauty, rich biodiversity, and unique underwater experiences make it a destination like no other.

Raja Ampat, Indonesia: Discovering Unparallelled Marine Biodiversity in Remote and Pristine Waters

Raja Ampat is located in the heart of the Coral Triangle, an area known as the epicentre of marine biodiversity. This remote archipelago consists of four main islands, Waigeo, Batanta, Salawati, and Misool, along with hundreds of smaller islands and islets. The unique geography of Raja Ampat, with its deep channels and nutrient-rich upwellings, creates the perfect conditions for the growth of coral reefs and supports a rich and diverse marine ecosystem.

The crystal-clear waters of Raja Ampat are home to thousands of species of fish and hundreds of species of coral, making it one of the most biodiverse marine habitats on the planet. From colourful clownfish to elusive reef sharks, the waters of Raja Ampat are teeming with life. The sheer abundance and variety of marine species in this region are unparallelled, making every dive a truly awe-inspiring experience.

Raja Ampat's pristine beaches and stunning limestone cliffs provide a picturesque backdrop to the underwater wonders. The islands are covered in lush greenery, with dense rainforests and mangrove forests that are home to a wide range of terrestrial species. The remote and untouched nature of Raja Ampat ensures the preservation of its natural beauty, making it a haven for wildlife and nature enthusiasts.

Exploring the Coral Reefs of Raja Ampat

As you dive into the crystal-clear waters of Raja Ampat, you'll be transported to a world of vibrant colours and abundant marine life. The coral reefs of Raja Ampat are a sight to behold, with their intricate formations and stunning variety of corals. From massive table corals to delicate branching corals, the reefs are a testament to nature's artistry.

One of the most famous dive sites in Raja Ampat is known as "The Passage." This narrow channel is lined with towering limestone cliffs and is home to an incredible diversity of marine life. As you swim through the passage, you will encounter schools of fish, colourful soft corals, and even the elusive walking shark. The Passage is just one of many dive sites in Raja Ampat that offer a unique and unforgettable underwater experience.

For snorkelers, the shallow reefs of Raja Ampat provide an opportunity to get up close and personal with the marine life. The crystal-clear waters make it easy to spot colourful fish, playful turtles, and even small reef sharks. Snorkelling in Raja Ampat is like floating in an aquarium, surrounded by a symphony of colours and marine life.

Best Time to Visit Raja Ampat

Raja Ampat can be visited year-round, but the best time to visit depends on your preferences and what you hope to see. The dry season, from October to April, offers calm seas and good visibility for diving and snorkelling. During this time, the water temperature is warm and comfortable, making it ideal for spending long hours in the water.

The wet season, from May to September, brings occasional rain showers and stronger currents. While the visibility may not be as good during this time, the reefs are often at their most vibrant and colourful. The wet season also coincides with the mating season for some species, such as manta rays, offering a unique opportunity to witness their courtship displays.

Raja Ampat promises an unforgettable experience that will leave you in awe of the wonders of the underwater world.

Belize Barrier Reef, Belize: Exploring a UNESCO World Heritage Site Teeming With Marine Life

Being recognised by UNESCO as a World Heritage Site, the Belize Barrier Reef is extremely significant. It is not just a marvel of nature but also an essential ecosystem that is home to a wide variety of marine species.

This reef system is a crucial habitat for numerous species, including endangered ones. Its preservation is essential for the overall health of the oceans and the planet.

The UNESCO designation acknowledges the outstanding universal value of the Belize Barrier Reef. It serves as a global recognition of its exceptional beauty, biodiversity, and ecological significance. The protection and preservation of this reef are important not only for Belize but also for the entire world.

Biodiversity and Marine Life in the Belize Barrier Reef

The Belize Barrier Reef is a treasure trove of biodiversity. It is home to an astounding array of marine species, making it a paradise for nature enthusiasts and underwater photographers. The reef supports over 500 species of fish, 65 species of coral, and numerous other marine organisms.

One of the most iconic creatures found in the Belize Barrier Reef is the magnificent whale shark. These gentle giants migrate to the area between April and June, offering a thrilling encounter for divers. Alongside the whale sharks, you will also encounter vibrant parrotfish, graceful sea turtles, and elusive seahorses, among many other fascinating species.

Top Dive Sites in the Belize Barrier Reef

The Belize Barrier Reef is renowned for its exceptional dive sites. Here are some of the top spots that should be on every diver's bucket list:

- **The Great Blue Hole:** This iconic dive site is a natural wonder characterized by a massive underwater sinkhole. Descending into the depths of the Great Blue Hole is an awe-inspiring experience as you explore intricate stalactite formations and encounter various species of sharks.

- **Hol Chan Marine Reserve:** Located near Ambergris Caye, this marine reserve is teeming with marine life. Dive into the crystal-clear waters and swim alongside schools of colourful fish, graceful rays, and even friendly nurse sharks.

- **Glover's Reef Atoll:** This remote and pristine atoll offers an unforgettable diving experience. Explore the vibrant coral walls, encounter massive groupers, and drift along the currents while being surrounded by a myriad of marine life.

Best Time to Visit the Belize Barrier Reef

The Belize Barrier Reef can be visited year-round, but the best time to experience optimal conditions for diving and snorkelling is during the dry season, which runs from

November to April. The weather is generally mild, and visibility underwater is excellent during this period.

However, if you prefer to avoid crowds and enjoy lower rates, visiting during the shoulder seasons (May to June and September to October) can still provide a fantastic experience. Just be prepared for occasional showers and slightly reduced visibility.

With its stunning underwater landscapes and diverse marine life, the Belize Barrier Reef is a must-visit destination for anyone seeking a truly mesmerizing experience.

Chapter 5:

Off the Beaten Path:

Hidden Gems and Unique

Adventures

Remote and Unexplored Territories

Svalbard, Norway: Exploring the Arctic Wilderness and Encountering Polar Bears and Glaciers

Svalbard is a remote archipelago situated in the Arctic Ocean, halfway between mainland Norway and the North Pole. Comprising four main islands and numerous smaller ones, it is characterised by its rugged mountains, icy fjords, and vast expanses of glaciers. The unique geography of Svalbard offers a diverse range of landscapes, from snow-covered peaks to deep valleys and frozen tundras.

The climate in Svalbard is classified as Arctic, with long, cold winters and short, cool summers. The extreme cold and limited daylight during the winter months create a harsh environment, but it also provides the perfect conditions for witnessing the mesmerizing Northern Lights.

Wildlife of Svalbard

Svalbard is home to a remarkable array of wildlife adapted to survive in one of the most challenging environments on Earth. From reindeer grazing on the tundra to Arctic foxes darting across the icy landscape, the archipelago offers a unique opportunity to observe these magnificent creatures up close.

The polar bear is Svalbard's most famous inhabitant. One of the best locations on Earth to witness these magnificent animals in their native environment is Svalbard, where their number is estimated to be around 3,000. Nonetheless, due to their protected status, one must exercise caution and respect when approaching a polar bear.

Other notable wildlife species found in Svalbard include walruses, seals, and a wide variety of seabirds. The archipelago is also a breeding ground for several migratory bird species, making it a paradise for birdwatchers.

Polar Bears in Svalbard

Svalbard is renowned for its polar bear population, and encountering these magnificent creatures in their natural habitat is an unforgettable experience. The archipelago provides a vital habitat for polar bears, as the sea ice serves as a hunting ground for their primary prey, seals.

To ensure the safety of both visitors and polar bears, strict regulations are in place to govern polar bear encounters. Guided tours are the best way to observe these magnificent creatures up close, as experienced guides know how to approach them safely and responsibly. These tours offer a unique opportunity to learn about the behaviour and conservation efforts surrounding polar bears.

Remember, polar bears are wild animals, and it is important to respect their space and observe them from a safe distance. Your encounter with a polar bear in Svalbard is a rare privilege, and by following the guidelines, you can help protect these incredible creatures for future generations.

Glaciers and Ice Caves in Svalbard

Svalbard is a land of ice and glaciers, with most of its landmass covered in ice. The archipelago boasts a vast number of glaciers, each with its own unique characteristics and stunning beauty. From the massive Austfonna Glacier, one of the largest in Europe, to the intricate ice formations of the Kongsbreen Glacier, exploring these frozen wonders is a once-in-a-lifetime experience.

One of the most fascinating aspects of the glaciers in Svalbard is the presence of ice caves. These natural formations, sculpted by centuries of ice and water, offer a glimpse into an otherworldly realm. Walking through the shimmering blue tunnels of an ice cave is like stepping into a fairy tale, with the light filtering through the translucent ice creating a mesmerizing spectacle.

Exploring the glaciers and ice caves of Svalbard requires proper equipment and guidance, as the terrain can be treacherous. Joining a guided tour with experienced mountaineers ensures both your safety and the preservation of these delicate natural wonders.

How to get To Svalbard

Travelling to Svalbard is a very adventurous trip. The Archipelago is accessible by air, with regular flights from Oslo, Norway. The main gateway to Svalbard is Longyearbyen, the largest settlement on the archipelago. From there, you can explore the other islands and embark on various excursions.

It is important to note that all visitors to Svalbard must have comprehensive travel insurance, including evacuation coverage. The remote location and challenging environment make it crucial to have proper insurance in case of emergencies.

Pack your warmest clothes and get ready for an adventure of a lifetime in Svalbard, Norway. The Arctic is waiting to be explored, and it is a journey you won't soon forget.

Socotra Island, Yemen: Discovering a Surreal Landscape With Unique Flora and Fauna

Socotra Island boasts a landscape that is straight out of a fantasy novel. As you set foot on this enchanting island, you will be immediately captivated by its otherworldly beauty. The island is dominated by towering limestone cliffs that reach up to 1,500 meters in height, creating a dramatic backdrop against the azure waters of the Arabian Sea. These cliffs provide a stunning contrast to the lush green valleys and deep canyons that dot the island, making Socotra a photographer's dream.

But it is the unique rock formations that truly set Socotra apart. The island is home to a series of "karsts," which are limestone formations that have been eroded over thousands of years, resulting in a surreal landscape of pinnacles, caves, and sinkholes. These karsts give Socotra an otherworldly feel as if you have stepped into a different dimension.

Flora and Fauna of Socotra Island

What makes Socotra Island truly special is its incredible biodiversity. Known as the "Galapagos of the Indian Ocean," this remote island is home to hundreds of endemic species found nowhere else on Earth. The isolation of Socotra, combined with its unique climate, has allowed these species to evolve in isolation for millions of years, resulting in a truly unique ecosystem.

One of the most iconic species found on Socotra Island is the Dragon's Blood Tree (*Dracaena cinnabari*). This strange-looking tree has a thick, umbrella-shaped canopy and a blood-red resin that oozes from its bark, giving it its distinctive name. The Dragon's Blood Tree is not only a symbol of Socotra Island but also a living testament to the island's ancient and isolated past.

Another fascinating plant species found on Socotra is the Bottle Tree (*Adenium obesum*). As the name suggests, these trees have a unique bottle-like shape, with a swollen trunk and branches that resemble the curves of a water bottle. The Bottle Trees are scattered across the landscape, adding to the surreal and alien-like atmosphere of Socotra Island.

Endemic Species Found on Socotra Island

Socotra Island is a haven for endemic species, with a remarkable number of plants and animals found nowhere else on the planet. In fact, less than half of the plant species on Socotra are endemic, making it one of the richest and most unique floras in the world. These endemic species have evolved in isolation on the island, adapting to its harsh and arid conditions over millions of years.

Apart from the Dragon's Blood Tree and the Bottle Tree, Socotra is also home to other endemic plant species such as the Socotra Fig (*Dorstenia gigas*), the Socotra Frankincense Tree (*Boswellia socotrana*), and the Socotra

Desert Rose (*Adenium socotranum*). Each of these species has its own unique adaptations to survive in the dry and rugged landscape of Socotra Island.

When it comes to fauna, Socotra is equally impressive. The island is home to a variety of endemic bird species, including the Socotra Starling (*Onychognathus frater*), the Socotra Sunbird (*Cinnyris socotranus*), and the Socotra Bunting (*Emberiza socotrana*). These birds have evolved in isolation on Socotra, resulting in distinct and unique populations that cannot be found anywhere else in the world.

How to get To Socotra Island

A Trip to Socotra Island is filled with non-ending adventure. Due to its remote location and limited transportation options, reaching the island requires careful planning and a sense of adventure. The most common way to reach Socotra is by flying from the Yemeni capital, Sana'a, or the Emirati city of Abu Dhabi.

Best Time to Visit Socotra Island

The best time to visit Socotra Island is during the cooler months of October to April, when the temperatures are milder and more pleasant. During these months, the island experiences a dry season, with little to no rainfall, making it ideal for outdoor activities and exploring the diverse landscapes.

However, if you are interested in witnessing the island's unique flora in full bloom, the months of February to

April are the best time to visit. During this time, Socotra comes alive with vibrant colours as various plant species, including the Dragon's Blood Trees, burst into bloom, creating a truly magical atmosphere.

Socotra Island is waiting to be discovered, offering a once-in-a-lifetime experience that will leave you in awe of the wonders of nature.

Bhutan: Immersing in the Tranquillity of the Himalayas and Exploring Ancient Monasteries

Bhutan's unique location in the Himalayas offers visitors a chance to witness some of the most breathtaking natural landscapes in the world. From snow-capped mountains to lush valleys, this country is a paradise for nature lovers. The pristine forests that cover Bhutan are home to a rich diversity of flora and fauna, some of which are found nowhere else on earth. Trekking through these forests, you will encounter rare species like the takin, Bhutan's national animal, and the elusive snow leopard.

As you venture further into the mountains, you will be rewarded with awe-inspiring vistas from the numerous mountain passes that dot the landscape. Fortress Monastery offers panoramic views of the Himalayan peaks on a clear day. The Chele La Pass, the highest motorable pass in Bhutan, provides a breathtaking vista of the Paro and Haa valleys. These majestic mountains and valleys are a testament to the raw beauty of Bhutan and will leave you in awe of nature's grandeur.

Bhutan's Ancient Monasteries and Their Significance

Bhutan's monasteries, bearing witness to centuries of devotion, provide a glimpse into the spiritual essence of this enchanting country. Each monastery holds its own unique charm and religious significance, adding to the rich cultural tapestry of Bhutan.

The iconic Tiger's Nest Monastery, also known as Paro Taktsang, is perhaps the most famous of them all. Perched precariously on a cliffside, it is said to be the meditation site of Guru Rinpoche, the founder of Bhutanese Buddhism. A visit to this monastery is not only a spiritual pilgrimage but also a test of endurance as you hike up the steep trail that leads to its entrance.

The second oldest and second largest dzong in Bhutan, Punakha Dzong, is another monastery of immense significance. This architectural wonder of a fortress-monastery sits at the meeting point of the Pho Chhu and Mo Chhu rivers. The exquisite paintings and detailed woodwork that cover the walls of Punakha Dzong are examples of Bhutanese artists' skill.

Experiencing the Tranquillity and Spirituality of Bhutan's Monastic Life

For those seeking a deeper spiritual experience, Bhutan offers the opportunity to stay in monasteries and immerse oneself in the peaceful and disciplined life of the monks. Several monasteries in Bhutan offer the chance to participate in meditation retreats and engage in spiritual practices under the guidance of experienced monks.

Cheri Monastery, located near Thimphu, is one such monastery that welcomes visitors seeking spiritual solace. Set in a serene environment, this monastery provides a perfect atmosphere for meditation and reflection. The Neyphug Monastery, located in a remote valley, is another hidden gem that offers a peaceful retreat away from the hustle and bustle of everyday life.

Let the tranquillity of the Himalayas and the ancient monasteries transport you into a world of inner peace and spiritual awakening. Bhutan awaits, ready to captivate your heart and soul.

Quirky and Unusual Destinations

Salar de Uyuni, Bolivia: Marvelling at the World's Largest Salt Flat, a Surreal Mirror During the Wet Season

During the wet season, Salar de Uyuni undergoes a surreal transformation that is nothing short of breathtaking. As the rainy season begins in December and extends through March, the salt flat becomes partially flooded, creating a mirror-like effect that is truly mesmerizing. The thin layer of water on the salt crust reflects the sky with such clarity that it becomes challenging to distinguish between the real and the mirrored world.

This ethereal mirror effect opens up a whole new realm of photographic opportunities, allowing you to capture stunning images that defy reality. The reflections of the clouds, mountains, and even the occasional group of flamingos create a dreamlike atmosphere that transports you to another dimension. The symphony of colours and textures, combined with the surreal reflections, make for a truly unforgettable experience.

The transformation of Salar de Uyuni during the wet season is not only visually stunning but also brings an added element of adventure. The flooded salt flat creates a unique and challenging terrain to navigate, with the water creating unexpected patterns and textures on the surface. It's like walking on a delicate, ever-changing canvas that requires careful navigation and a sense of wonder.

The Unique Geological Features of Salar de Uyuni

Salar de Uyuni is not just a salt flat; it is a geological wonder that holds a fascinating history within its crystalline landscape. The salt flat was formed as a result of the evaporation of prehistoric lakes, leaving behind a thick layer of salt and minerals. This geological process, spanning millions of years, has created a unique and captivating terrain that draws visitors from all around the world.

Beneath the salt crust lies a vast reserve of lithium, making Salar de Uyuni a significant source of this valuable mineral. The salt flat also contains other minerals, such as potassium and magnesium, which contribute to its unique composition. The geological diversity of the area, combined with the stunning visual spectacle, makes for an awe-inspiring experience.

In addition to the salt crust, Salar de Uyuni is also home to several other geological formations that add to its allure. From volcanic islands rising out of the salt flat to geysers and hot springs, the salt flat offers a myriad of natural wonders to explore. These geological features further enhance the surreal and otherworldly atmosphere, creating a truly immersive experience.

Cultural Significance and History of the Salt Flat

Beyond its natural beauty, Salar de Uyuni holds immense cultural significance for the people of Bolivia. The salt flat has been an integral part of the country's history and heritage, shaping the lives and traditions of the local communities.

For centuries, the salt flat has been a vital source of salt for the surrounding region. The locals have developed unique methods of harvesting salt, passing down their knowledge and techniques from generation to generation. Today, salt mining is still an essential economic activity in the area, and you can witness the traditional methods used by salt miners.

Salar de Uyuni is also steeped in folklore and legends that have been passed down through the ages. The salt flat is believed to be the birthplace of the Inca civilisation, and many indigenous communities consider it a sacred place.

Best Time to Visit Salar de Uyuni

The best time to visit Salar de Uyuni largely depends on the experience you seek. The wet season, from December to March, offers the surreal mirror effect created by the flooded salt flat. This is the time when the landscape transforms into a breathtaking spectacle, with the reflections adding a magical touch to the already stunning scenery.

On the other hand, the dry season, from April to November, offers a different perspective of Salar de Uyuni. During this time, the salt flat is mostly dry, revealing its vast expanse of white salt crust. The dry season provides an opportunity to witness the unique geological features in greater detail, as well as explore the surrounding attractions, such as the volcanoes and geysers.

It is important to note that the weather conditions in Salar de Uyuni can be extreme, with temperatures ranging from below-freezing to scorching heat. The high altitude also adds to the challenge, with thinner air and increased risk of altitude sickness. It is advisable to check the weather forecast and plan accordingly, dressing in layers and carrying appropriate gear to adapt to changing conditions.

Salar de Uyuni, Bolivia, is a destination that defies imagination and leaves visitors in awe of its natural beauty and surreal landscapes. Brace yourself for an unforgettable experience that will transport you to a world where reality and illusion blend seamlessly and the beauty of nature knows no bounds.

Cappadocia, Turkey: Witnessing the Unique Rock Formations and Hot Air Balloon Rides at Sunrise

Cappadocia is a geological wonderland shaped by millions of years of volcanic activity and erosion. The region's unique landscape is the result of volcanic ash and lava being shaped into cones, pillars, and mushroom-like formations known as "fairy chimneys." These fairy chimneys can be found scattered across the valleys, creating a surreal and almost magical atmosphere.

The soft, porous rock of Cappadocia's fairy chimneys has been carved by wind and water over centuries, resulting in intricate formations that seem to defy gravity. Some of these formations reach up to 130 feet in height, with their vibrant colours adding to the allure of the landscape.

The geological wonders of Cappadocia are not limited to above ground. The region is also known for its underground cities, which were carved out of the soft volcanic rock as early as the 8th century BC. Early Christians used these underground towns as hiding places when they were being persecuted. These historic cities are open for exploration today, giving tourists a window into the past.

Exploring the Rock Formations and Fairy Chimneys

One of the best ways to experience the rock formations and fairy chimneys of Cappadocia is by taking a hike through the valleys. The most popular valley for exploration is the Rose Valley, known for its stunning pink-hued rocks. As you walk through the valley, you'll come across hidden churches, cave dwellings, and breathtaking viewpoints that offer panoramic views of the surrounding landscape.

The Göreme Open Air Museum, a UNESCO World Heritage Site, is another place you really must see. There are numerous rock-cut chapels with exquisite frescoes inside this outdoor museum. You may get a taste of the rich history and cultural legacy of the area by touring these historic churches.

For a more adventurous experience, consider taking a hot air balloon ride over the rock formations. As you float above the fairy chimneys, you'll get a bird's-eye view of the unique landscape below. The colours, shapes, and textures of Cappadocia's rock formations are truly awe-inspiring when seen from above.

Hot Air Balloon Rides Over Cappadocia

One of the most iconic experiences in Cappadocia is taking a hot air balloon ride at sunrise. As the first rays of light illuminate the surreal landscape, hundreds of colourful hot air balloons take flight, creating a truly magical scene. The calm and peaceful atmosphere at sunrise, combined with the breathtaking views, make this experience unforgettable.

Hot air balloon rides in Cappadocia are typically conducted early in the morning when the weather conditions are most favourable. The balloons gently lift off the ground, carrying passengers high above the rock formations and valleys. The serene and quiet nature of the experience allows you to fully immerse yourself in the beauty of Cappadocia.

From its geological wonders to its rich history and delicious cuisine, Cappadocia has something to offer every traveller. So go on an adventure and prepare to witness the breathtaking beauty of Turkey's hidden gem.

The Wave, Arizona, USA: Hiking Through Otherworldly Sandstone Formations in the Desert

The Wave is a geological marvel that showcases the power of nature's artistic touch. Formed over millions of years, the sandstone formations bear witness to the transformative forces of wind and water. The result is a mesmerizing landscape that resembles a frozen ocean wave frozen in time. The swirling patterns and contoured layers create a visual feast for the eyes, with each step revealing a new masterpiece of nature's craftsmanship.

The sandstone at The Wave is composed of various minerals, including iron oxide and manganese oxide, which give rise to the vibrant colours that adorn the formations. From deep reds to creamy whites, the palette of hues is a testament to the geological processes that shaped this unique landscape. The interplay of sunlight and shadow further accentuates the intricate textures, creating a surreal and ethereal atmosphere.

To access The Wave, you'll need to obtain a permit, as the area has limited access to preserve its natural beauty and ensure the sustainability of the fragile ecosystem. The Bureau of Land Management (BLM) issues a limited number of permits each day through an online lottery system. It's important to plan ahead and apply for the lottery well in advance, as demand for permits is high.

The hike to The Wave is not for the faint of heart, but it's definitely worth the effort. The trail is approximately 6 miles round trip and can be quite challenging due to the rugged terrain and lack of signage. It's crucial to be well-prepared, bring plenty of water, wear sturdy hiking boots, and have a good map or GPS device.

The best time to visit The Wave is during spring and fall when temperatures are more moderate. Summers can be scorching, so it's advisable to avoid hiking during this time unless you're experienced and prepared for extreme heat. Winter can also bring cold temperatures, so dressing in layers is essential.

The unique sandstone formations, vibrant colours, and serene atmosphere make it a must-visit destination for outdoor enthusiasts.

Antarctica: Experiencing the Vast Icy Landscapes and Encountering Penguins and Seals

Antarctica, the southernmost continent on Earth, remains one of the most remote and pristine destinations in the world. Planning a trip to this magnificent land requires careful consideration and preparation. Before setting foot on this icy paradise, it is essential to gather information about the best time to visit, transportation options, wildlife encounters, activities, safety guidelines, and sustainable tourism practices.

When planning your trip, it's crucial to choose the right time of year to visit Antarctica. The continent experiences extreme weather conditions, with temperatures dropping well below freezing and strong winds blowing across the icy landscapes. The summer months, from November to March, offer the best window for exploration, with milder temperatures and longer daylight hours. During this time, you can witness the mesmerizing sight of icebergs calving, penguin colonies bustling with activity, and whales migrating through the Antarctic waters.

Best Time to Visit Antarctica

Travelling to Antarctica requires careful consideration of the best time to visit this pristine continent. The summer months, from November to March, offer the most favourable conditions for exploration. During this time, the temperature is relatively milder, ranging from -2°C to 8°C (28°F to 46°F), making it more bearable for travellers. Additionally, the longer daylight hours provide ample time to immerse yourself in the breathtaking beauty of Antarctica.

November marks the beginning of the summer season, and it's a fantastic time to witness the arrival of numerous bird species, such as albatrosses and petrels, to their breeding grounds. December is an excellent month to observe penguins tending to their chicks, as well as to experience the mesmerizing sight of icebergs calving. January and February are the peak months for wildlife encounters, with penguin colonies bustling with activity and whales making their annual migration through the Antarctic waters. March, the end of the summer season, offers a unique opportunity to witness the stunning autumn hues and bid farewell to Antarctica as winter approaches.

Wildlife Encounters in Antarctica: Penguins, Seals, and Whales

One of the main highlights of a trip to Antarctica is the opportunity to encounter its incredible wildlife. The continent is home to a diverse array of species, including penguins, seals, and whales. These charismatic creatures have adapted to survive in the extreme conditions of Antarctica and offer a truly unforgettable experience for visitors.

Penguins are undoubtedly the stars of Antarctica, and encountering these adorable birds in their natural habitat is a truly magical experience. Adélie, Chinstrap, and Gentoo penguins are the most common species found in the region, each with its unique characteristics and behaviours. From witnessing their comical waddle across the ice to observing their feeding and breeding rituals, penguins never fail to captivate and entertain.

Seals are another fascinating group of animals that call Antarctica home. Weddell seals, Antarctic fur seals, and crabeater seals can be spotted along the Antarctic coastline, often lounging on ice floes or diving into the frigid waters. Observing these graceful creatures in their natural environment is a humbling experience as you witness their agility and adaptability to harsh conditions.

Whale enthusiasts will also be delighted by the abundance of marine mammals in Antarctica. The Southern Ocean surrounding the continent is a feeding ground for several whale species, including humpback, minke, and orca whales. Witnessing these majestic creatures breach or hearing their haunting songs echoing through the icy waters is a truly mesmerizing sight.

Visit Antarctica and prepare to be amazed by the vast icy landscapes and the fascinating creatures that call this frozen wonderland home.

Sahara Desert, Morocco: Embarking on Camel Treks and Camping under the Stars in the Dunes

The Sahara Desert is not just a vast expanse of sand; it is a unique ecosystem teeming with life and surprises. Despite its harsh conditions, the desert is home to a wide array of flora and fauna that have adapted to survive in this arid environment.

The desert's most iconic inhabitants are the camels, also known as the "ships of the desert." These magnificent creatures can endure the scorching heat and sandstorms, making them the perfect companions for exploring the dunes. As you embark on a camel trek, you'll witness the desert come alive with creatures like the fennec fox, desert monitor lizard, and various species of birds.

But it is not just the animal life that makes the Sahara Desert unique. The desert is also scattered with oases, providing a respite from the harsh conditions. These lush pockets of green are home to date palm trees and other plants that thrive in the desert's limited water supply. Exploring these oases is like discovering hidden paradises in the midst of a barren landscape.

Camel Trekking in the Sahara Desert

One of the most unforgettable experiences in the Sahara Desert is embarking on a camel trek. As you mount your camel and set off into the vast expanse of sand, you'll feel a sense of freedom and adventure like never before.

Camels are the perfect companions for traversing the dunes. Their padded feet allow them to walk effortlessly on the shifting sands, and their ability to store water and withstand extreme temperatures makes them well-suited for desert travel.

During your camel trek, you'll be guided by experienced local guides who have an intimate knowledge of the desert. They will lead you through towering dunes, ancient caravan routes, and hidden valleys, revealing the secrets of the desert along the way.

Camp Under the Stars in the Sahara Desert

Imagine lying under a blanket of stars, far away from the hustle and bustle of city life. In the Sahara Desert, camping under the stars is not just a dream; it's a reality that will leave you in awe of the universe.

As night falls in the desert, the sky transforms into a celestial masterpiece. With minimal light pollution, the stars shine brightly, creating a breathtaking spectacle. Gazing up at the night sky, you'll feel a sense of insignificance and wonder, realizing just how vast and mysterious the universe is.

Camping in the Sahara Desert is a truly immersive experience. You'll sleep in traditional Berber tents, surrounded by the tranquillity of the desert. The rhythmic sound of the wind and the soft glow of the stars will lull you into a peaceful slumber, far away from the noise and distractions of everyday life.

In the morning, as the first rays of sunlight pierce the horizon, you'll witness a magical transformation. The desert, bathed in golden light, comes alive with a symphony of colours. The contrast between the cool desert air and the warmth of the sun on your skin is invigorating, filling you with a sense of renewal and gratitude.

Must-Visit Destinations in the Sahara Desert

The Sahara Desert stretches across several countries, but Morocco offers some of the most captivating destinations to explore. Here are a few must-visit places in the Moroccan Sahara:

- **Merzouga:** Located on the edge of the Erg Chebbi dunes, Merzouga is a popular starting point for camel treks and desert excursions. The towering sand dunes offer a surreal backdrop, and the nearby village provides an opportunity to immerse yourself in the local culture.

- **Zagora:** Situated at the gateway to the Sahara Desert, Zagora is known for its stunning sunsets and ancient kasbahs. Take a camel trek to explore the surrounding dunes or visit the Draa Valley, famous for its date palm groves and picturesque landscapes.

- **M'Hamid El Ghizlane:** For a more off-the-beaten-path experience, head to M'Hamid El Ghizlane. This remote desert town offers a peaceful escape from the crowds, allowing you to truly immerse yourself in the beauty of the Sahara Desert.

These destinations, among many others, offer a glimpse into the diverse landscapes and cultures of the Sahara Desert.

Best Time to Visit the Sahara Desert

The best time to visit the Sahara Desert is during the cooler months, from October to April. During this time, temperatures are more moderate, making it more comfortable for exploration and camel treks.

In the winter months, from December to February, the desert can get quite cold, especially at night. It's important to pack warm clothing and sleeping bags to ensure your comfort during camping.

During the summer months, from May to September, the desert experiences extremely high temperatures, often exceeding 40 degrees Celsius (104 degrees Fahrenheit). The heat can be challenging to bear, so it is advisable to avoid visiting during this time unless you are well-prepared and can handle the extreme conditions.

It is time to leave behind the noise of modern civilisation and venture into the enchanting world of the Sahara Desert. Let the rhythmic sway of the camels and the timeless beauty of the desert guide you on a journey that will forever be etched in your memory. The Sahara Desert awaits, ready to captivate your heart and soul.

Mount Kilimanjaro, Tanzania: Climb Africa's Highest Peak and Witness Breathtaking Vistas

Mount Kilimanjaro, located in northeastern Tanzania, is the highest peak in Africa and the tallest freestanding mountain in the world. It is made up of Kibo, Mawenzi, and Shira, three separate volcanic cones. Part of the UNESCO World Heritage Site Kilimanjaro National Park, the peak is a dormant volcano. Climbers from all over the world are drawn to Kilimanjaro in an attempt to reach its lofty peak and take in its exceptional beauty.

The name "Kilimanjaro" is derived from the Swahili word "Kilima," meaning "mountain," and the Chagga word "Njaro," meaning "whiteness." This name perfectly captures the essence of the mountain, with its snow-capped peak standing in stark contrast to the surrounding African landscape.

Climbing Routes on Mount Kilimanjaro

There are various climbing routes available atop Mount Kilimanjaro, each with special characteristics and difficulties. The Northern Circuit, the Lemosho, Rongai, Machame, and Marangu circuits are the most travelled routes. Each route varies in terms of duration, difficulty, and scenery, allowing climbers to choose the one that best suits their preferences and capabilities.

The Marangu Route, also known as the "Coca-Cola Route," is the most straightforward and well-established route on the mountain. It offers hut accommodations along the way, providing climbers with a more comfortable experience. However, this route is also the busiest, making it less ideal for those seeking a more secluded adventure.

The Machame Route, often referred to as the "Whiskey Route," is a more challenging option that takes climbers through diverse landscapes, including lush rainforests, steep cliffs, and alpine deserts. This path is well-known for its picturesque splendour and provides amazing vistas. However, because of its high elevation, it calls for a decent degree of fitness and acclimatization.

The Lemosho Route is considered one of the most scenic routes on Mount Kilimanjaro, offering panoramic views of the surrounding landscapes. This route is longer and more remote, allowing for better acclimatisation and a higher chance of reaching the summit. It is recommended for climbers who prefer a quieter and less crowded experience.

The Rongai Route approaches the mountain from the northeast and is known for its wilderness and solitude. It is a less crowded route that offers a unique perspective of the mountain and its surrounding wilderness. This route is often chosen by those seeking a quieter and more remote experience.

The Northern Circuit is the newest and longest route on Mount Kilimanjaro, offering a complete circumnavigation of the mountain. This route provides ample time for acclimatisation and offers stunning views of the northern slopes of the mountain. It is a less crowded route and is suitable for climbers who prefer a longer and more challenging adventure.

Witnessing Breathtaking Vistas From the Summit

Reaching the summit of Mount Kilimanjaro is a moment of unparallelled beauty and triumph. As you stand on the summit of Uhuru Peak, you will be rewarded with breathtaking vistas that stretch as far as the eye can see. The snow-capped peak, the vast African plains, and the surrounding mountains create a panoramic view that is nothing short of awe-inspiring.

The sunrise from the summit is a particularly magical moment. As the first rays of sunlight illuminate the landscape, the world below comes alive with hues of gold and orange. The vastness of Africa unfolds before you, offering a perspective that few have the privilege to witness. It is a sight that will leave you humbled and in awe of the beauty of our planet.

Remember to savour every moment of your climb, take in the breathtaking views, and celebrate your achievements along the way. Climbing Mount Kilimanjaro is not just about reaching the summit; it is about embracing the journey and immersing yourself in the wonders of Africa.

Chapter 6:

Culinary Journeys:

Gastronomic Delights

Around the World

Food Capitals and Culinary Experiences

Bangkok, Thailand: Indulging in Vibrant Street Food and Flavours of Thai Cuisine

Bangkok's street food scene is a sensory feast that attracts both locals and tourists alike. The city's vibrant street markets offer a treasure trove of culinary delights, where you can witness the magic of Thai cooking right before your eyes. From the sizzle of the woks to the aromatic spices wafting through the air, there's an undeniable energy that makes Bangkok's street food experience truly unique.

Exploring the Flavours of Thai Cuisine

Thai cuisine is a harmonious blend of flavours, combining the richness of coconut milk, the tanginess of lime, the heat of chili peppers, and the freshness of herbs. The balance of these elements creates a symphony of tastes that is both complex and satisfying. From the creamy and aromatic Massaman curry to the zesty and fragrant Som Tam salad, Thai cuisine offers a diverse range of flavours that cater to all taste preferences.

Must-Try Street Food in Bangkok

When it comes to street food in Bangkok, the options are endless. One must-try dish is Pad Thai, a stir-fried noodle dish that showcases the perfect marriage of sweet, sour, and savoury flavours. Another popular choice is Tom Yum soup, a spicy and tangy broth infused with fragrant herbs and plump shrimp. For those seeking a fiery kick, the green curry is a must-try, with its aromatic blend of spices and creamy coconut milk.

Popular Thai Dishes and Their Unique Flavours

Thai cuisine is as diverse as the country itself, with each region offering its own set of signature dishes. The North is renowned for its fiery and delicious foods like Gaeng Som, a tangy and sour curry, while the North is home to delicacies like Khao Soi, a rich and creamy curry noodle soup. Famous foods like Pla Rad Prik, a deep-fried fish covered in chili sauce, and Pad Kra Pao, a fiery stir-fry with holy basil, can be found in central Thailand. Every dish highlights the distinctive tastes and components of the place in which it is made.

Where to Find the Best Street Food in Bangkok

To truly experience the best of Bangkok's street food, head to the city's bustling markets and hidden alleyways. The famous Yaowarat Road in Chinatown is a food lover's paradise, with its endless rows of street vendors serving up everything from succulent grilled meats to delectable dim sum. For a more local experience, check out the Bang Rak neighbourhood, known for its vibrant street food scene and authentic Thai flavours. And of course, no visit to Bangkok is complete without a trip to the iconic Chatuchak Weekend Market, where you can sample a wide variety of street food while browsing through the myriad of stalls.

Bangkok's vibrant street food scene is a culinary adventure like no other. The city offers a gastronomic journey that will delight your taste buds and ignite your passion for food. Go ahead and immerse yourself in the vibrant street food culture where every bite is a celebration of flavours.

Barcelona, Spain: Exploring the Culinary Diversity from Tapas to Innovative Michelin-starred Restaurants

Barcelona, Spain, is a culinary paradise that offers a delightful blend of traditional tapas and innovative Michelin-starred restaurants. Let us start with tapas, which are small plates of various dishes that are meant to be shared. These bite-sized culinary creations are the heart and soul of Spanish cuisine, and Barcelona is no exception. From classic patatas bravas (fried potatoes with spicy tomato sauce) to succulent gambas al ajillo (garlic shrimp), tapas bars in Barcelona offer a wide variety of options to satisfy any palate.

One of the most famous areas for tapas in Barcelona is the lively neighbourhood of El Born. Here, you can find charming narrow streets lined with tapas bars that serve up delectable bites. Don't miss out on trying the renowned pa amb tomàquet (bread with tomato), which is a simple yet incredibly tasty dish that perfectly represents Catalan cuisine.

Moving on to Michelin-starred restaurants, Barcelona boasts a thriving gastronomic scene that has attracted world-renowned chefs from all over the globe. These chefs have brought their innovative techniques and unique flavours to the city, creating an exciting fusion of traditional Catalan cuisine with international influences. One such example is the famous restaurant Tickets, owned by the acclaimed chef Albert Adrià.

Tickets offer an avant-garde dining experience where you can indulge in creative tapas that push the boundaries of gastronomy. From liquid olives to spherical olives, every dish at Tickets is a work of art that will leave you amazed.

If you are looking for a more traditional Michelin-starred experience, head over to Disfrutar, a restaurant that showcases modern interpretations of classic Catalan dishes. With its elegant ambiance and impeccable service, Disfrutar offers an unforgettable culinary journey that will transport you to gastronomic heaven.

Under the direction of famous chef Jordi Cruz, ABaC is another must-see Michelin-starred restaurant in Barcelona. This restaurant serves a delicious tasting menu, including only the best foods from Catalonia and beyond. Astonish yourself with the distinct tastes and flawless presentation of every dish.

In addition to tapas and Michelin-starred restaurants, Barcelona also boasts vibrant food markets where you can explore an array of local produce and delicacies. La Boqueria is one such market that offers a sensory overload of colours, aromas, and flavours. Here, you can sample fresh fruits, seafood, meats, and cheeses while immersing yourself in the vibrant atmosphere.

Exploring the culinary diversity in Barcelona is a gastronomic adventure like no other. From indulging in traditional tapas to experiencing innovative Michelin-starred dining, this city offers something for every food lover. So grab your fork and knife, and get ready to embark on a culinary journey that will leave you craving for more.

Oaxaca, Mexico: Delving Into the Rich Tapestry of Mexican Cuisine, From Mole to Mezcal

Oaxaca, Mexico, is a food lover's paradise, offering a rich tapestry of Mexican cuisine that is sure to tantalise your taste buds. From the famous mole to the unique flavours of mezcal, there is something for everyone to enjoy in this vibrant culinary destination.

Let us begin with mole, which is undoubtedly one of the most iconic dishes in Oaxacan cuisine. Mole is a complex sauce made from a variety of ingredients, including chili peppers, spices, nuts, seeds, and chocolate. The result is a thick, velvety sauce that can be served over meats, enchiladas, or even tamales.

Each region in Oaxaca has its own version of mole, with some variations being spicier or sweeter than others. Regardless of which type you try, you can expect an explosion of flavours that will leave you craving more. Another must-try in Oaxaca is mezcal, a traditional Mexican spirit made from the agave plant.

Mezcal has gained popularity in recent years due to its unique smoky flavour and artisanal production methods. Unlike its cousin, tequila, which is made from blue agave and primarily produced in the state of Jalisco, mezcal can be made from various types of agave and can be found throughout Mexico. However, Oaxaca is considered the capital of mezcal production, with many small-batch distilleries offering guided tours and tastings. Whether you prefer it neat or in a craft cocktail, mezcal is an experience that should not be missed.

Oaxacan cuisine offers much more than just mole and mezcal. The region is known for its abundance of fresh produce and traditional cooking techniques that have been passed down through generations. Zapotec indigenous communities play a significant role in preserving these culinary traditions, using ingredients such as corn, beans, squash, and herbs to create delicious dishes that reflect the local culture. One such example is tlayudas, a traditional Oaxacan dish that can best be described as a Mexican pizza. It starts with a large toasted tortilla spread with refried beans and topped with various ingredients such as grilled meat, cheese, avocado, and salsa. The combination of flavours and textures is simply mouthwatering.

For seafood lovers, Oaxaca's coastal regions offer an array of fresh and flavourful options. Whether it's ceviche made with marinated fish or shrimp tacos topped with tangy lime crema, you'll find plenty of seafood dishes to satisfy your cravings.

Exploring the street food scene in Oaxaca is also a must-do for any food enthusiast. From tacos al pastor dripping with juicy marinated pork to tamales wrapped in banana leaves and steamed to perfection, the street vendors in Oaxaca offer an endless selection of tasty treats that won't break the bank.

Oaxaca, Mexico, is a culinary gem that offers a wide range of delicious dishes and flavour. From the rich complexity of mole to the smoky allure of mezcal, there is no shortage of culinary delights to explore. So, prepare your taste buds for an unforgettable gastronomic adventure in Oaxaca!

Exotic Markets and Local Delicacies

Marrakech, Morocco: Wander Through the Bustling Souks and Savour Traditional Moroccan Dishes

Marrakech, Morocco, is a destination that truly captivates the senses. From the moment you step foot in this vibrant city, you will be swept away by its bustling souks, tantalizing aromas, and rich cultural heritage.

One of the highlights of visiting Marrakech is getting lost in the labyrinthine streets of its famous souks. These bustling marketplaces are a treasure trove of handcrafted goods, from intricately woven rugs to ornate ceramics and beautifully embroidered clothing.

After working up an appetite exploring the souks, make sure to indulge in some traditional Moroccan cuisine. The local dishes are a true feast for the taste buds, with flavours that are both exotic and comforting. One must-try dish is tagine, a slow-cooked stew that is typically made with tender meat, vegetables, and a blend of aromatic spices.

The fragrant combination of cinnamon, cumin, and saffron will transport you to another world with every bite. Another culinary delight is couscous, which is often served with succulent pieces of chicken or lamb and topped with a medley of vegetables. And let us not forget about the iconic Moroccan mint tea – a refreshing beverage that is steeped in tradition and enjoyed throughout the day.

In addition to exploring the souks and savouring delicious food, Marrakech offers a wealth of cultural and historical attractions. The city's most famous landmark is the Koutoubia Mosque, an architectural masterpiece that dates back to the 12th century. Its towering minaret can be seen from miles away and serves as a symbol of Marrakech's religious heritage.

Another must-visit site is the Bahia Palace, a stunning palace complex that showcases the opulence of Moroccan architecture and design. Take a stroll through its lush gardens and marvel at the intricate tilework and elaborate carvings.

For those seeking a respite from the hustle and bustle of the city, Marrakech also boasts several tranquil gardens and parks. The Majorelle Garden is a true oasis in the heart of Marrakech, with its vibrant blue buildings, exotic plants, and serene atmosphere. It was once owned by French painter Jacques Majorelle and later restored by fashion designer Yves Saint Laurent.

Another peaceful retreat is the Menara Gardens, which feature a large reflecting pool surrounded by olive groves – the perfect spot for a leisurely stroll or a picnic.

Marrakech, Morocco, is a destination that will enchant and inspire you. Prepare to be transported to another world as you immerse yourself in the sights, sounds, and flavours of Marrakech.

Tokyo, Japan: Explore Tsukiji Market and Taste Fresh Sushi and Street Snacks

Tokyo, Japan, is a vibrant and bustling city with so much to offer. One of the must-visit places in Tokyo is Tsukiji Market, a paradise for food lovers. If you're a sushi enthusiast or just someone who enjoys trying new and delicious street snacks, Tsukiji Market is the place to be.

Located in the Chuo ward of Tokyo, Tsukiji Market is the largest wholesale fish and seafood market in the world. It is renowned for its wide variety of fresh seafood, including some of the best sushi you'll ever taste. The market opens early in the morning, around 5:00 am, and it's recommended to go early to witness the lively auction of tuna and other seafood.

Once you enter Tsukiji Market, you'll find yourself surrounded by a bustling atmosphere filled with vendors selling all sorts of seafood and other culinary delights. The market is divided into two main sections: the inner market and the outer market. The inner market is where the wholesale auction takes place, and it is not open to the public until 10:00 am. However, if you want to experience the auction firsthand, you can arrive early and sign up for a guided tour. It's a unique opportunity to see how the professionals select and purchase their seafood.

The outer market is where all the action happens for tourists and locals alike. Here, you'll find an abundance of small shops and restaurants offering a wide range of food options. From sushi to sashimi, grilled seafood skewers to street snacks like takoyaki (octopus balls) and yakitori (grilled chicken skewers), there is something to satisfy every palate. One of the highlights of visiting Tsukiji Market is enjoying fresh sushi for breakfast.

Many sushi restaurants in the outer market offer omakase-style dining, where the chef selects and prepares a variety of sushi dishes for you. You can sit at the counter and watch as they expertly craft each piece using the freshest ingredients available.

If you are not a fan of raw fish, Tsukiji Market has plenty of other options to choose from. You can try tamagoyaki (Japanese omelette), tempura (battered and deep-fried seafood or vegetables), or even indulge in some matcha-flavoured treats like soft-serve ice cream or mochi.

While exploring Tsukiji Market, make sure to take your time and wander through the narrow alleys filled with shops selling kitchenware, Japanese snacks, and traditional crafts. You might stumble upon unique souvenirs or find yourself mesmerised by the beautiful displays of tea sets or lacquerware.

If you are in Tokyo and looking for an unforgettable culinary experience, Tsukiji Market is a must-visit destination. From its lively atmosphere to its incredible selection of fresh seafood and street snacks, this market will leave a lasting impression on your taste buds.

Fez, Morocco: Experiencing Spices' Vibrant Colours, Aromas, and Local Delicacies

Fez, Morocco, is a sensory delight for anyone who appreciates the vibrant colours, enticing aromas, and mouthwatering local delicacies that come from the world of spices. The city's rich history and cultural heritage make it the perfect destination to immerse yourself in the wonders of Moroccan cuisine.

When it comes to spices, Fez is a treasure trove. The medina, or old town, is home to numerous spice shops where you can explore a wide variety of spices that will awaken your senses. From aromatic cumin and coriander to fiery paprika and flavourful affron, you'll find an endless array of colours and aromas that will transport you to a world of exotic flavours.

One of the best ways to experience the spices of Fez is by visiting the famous spice market in the Medina. As you wander through the narrow alleys, your senses will be overwhelmed by the intoxicating scents emanating from the various stalls. You'll be greeted by friendly spice merchants who are more than happy to share their knowledge and expertise with you.

Moroccan cuisine is known for its bold flavours and unique combinations, and Fez is no exception. Whether you are indulging in a steaming bowl of traditional harira soup, savouring a tagine bursting with tender meat and vegetables, or enjoying a plate of fragrant couscous, you will be treated to a culinary experience like no other.

Fez is also famous for its sweet treats, and spices play a crucial role in many of these delectable desserts. From honey-soaked pastries filled with almonds and pistachios to aromatic orange blossom-flavoured cakes, your taste buds will be in for a treat. There is also the iconic mint tea, infused with fresh mint leaves and served in traditional silver teapots. It is the perfect way to end a meal or take a break from exploring the bustling streets of Fez.

Fez, Morocco, is a paradise for spice lovers. The city's vibrant colours, intoxicating aromas, and mouthwatering local delicacies make it a must-visit destination for anyone seeking an unforgettable culinary experience.

Wine Regions and Distinctive Beverage Experiences

Bordeaux, France: Tour Renowned Vineyards and Taste Exquisite Wines

Bordeaux, France, is an absolute must-visit destination for wine enthusiasts and connoisseurs alike. This beautiful region is renowned for its vineyards and the exquisite wines that are produced here.

One of the highlights of visiting Bordeaux is the opportunity to tour the renowned vineyards that dot the landscape. These vineyards have a rich history and are known for producing some of the finest wines in the world. From prestigious chateaux to family-owned estates, there is a wide variety of vineyards to choose from, each offering a unique tasting experience.

When you embark on a vineyard tour in Bordeaux, you will not only get a chance to see the stunning vineyards up close but also learn about the winemaking process from start to finish. Knowledgeable guides will take you through the vineyards, explaining the different grape varieties grown there and the factors that contribute to the quality of the wines.

You will also get to see the painstaking artistry that goes into each bottle by touring the vaults where the wines are matured. Obviously, a trip to Bordeaux would not be complete without partaking in wine tasting.

These tastings are a true delight for the senses, as you get to sample a wide range of wines, from bold reds to crisp whites and even some sweet dessert wines. The sommeliers and winemakers will guide you through each tasting, helping you understand the nuances of each wine and how it pairs with different foods.

In addition to touring vineyards and tasting wines, Bordeaux offers plenty of other attractions for visitors to enjoy. The city itself is steeped in history and boasts beautiful architecture, charming streets, and vibrant markets. Take a stroll along the Garonne River, explore the medieval streets of Saint-Émilion, or visit the iconic Cité du Vin, a museum dedicated to all things wine.

If you are planning a trip to Bordeaux, it is worth noting that the region has several wine routes that you can follow. These routes will take you through picturesque countryside, past vineyards, and charming villages, allowing you to soak in the beauty of the region while stopping at various wineries along the way.

Bordeaux is definitely a paradise for wine lovers. From touring renowned vineyards to tasting exquisite wines, this region offers an unforgettable experience for anyone who appreciates the art of winemaking. Whether you are a seasoned wine enthusiast or just starting your wine journey, Bordeaux will surely captivate your senses and leave you with lasting memories. Get ready for a wine-filled adventure in Bordeaux, France!

Napa Valley, USA: Exploring Picturesque Wineries and Experiencing Wine Tasting Tours

Napa Valley is known as the land of rolling vineyards and exquisite wines. If you are a wine enthusiast or simply someone who appreciates the beauty of picturesque wineries, then you are in for a treat.

Napa Valley, located in California, USA, is renowned for its world-class wineries and unforgettable wine-tasting tours. The valley boasts more than 400 wineries, each with its own unique charm and character. From historic family-owned estates to modern architectural marvels, there is something to suit every taste.

Whether you are a fan of bold reds or prefer crisp whites, Napa Valley has it all. The region is known for producing exceptional Cabernet Sauvignon, Chardonnay, and

Merlot, among other varietals. When it comes to exploring wineries, you have several options. Many wineries offer guided tours that take you through the vineyards, production facilities, and cellars.

You will get a chance to learn about the winemaking process and the art of wine aging. Some wineries even offer hands-on experiences where you can participate in grape picking or blending your own bottle of wine. If you prefer a more personalised experience, consider booking a private tasting with a winemaker. This allows you to delve deeper into the nuances of each wine and gain insights into the winemaking techniques employed. It is a fantastic opportunity to ask questions and expand your knowledge about the world of wine.

Apart from the wineries themselves, Napa Valley offers some breathtaking views and landscapes. As you drive through the valley, you will be treated to stunning vistas of rolling hills covered in vineyards. Many wineries have outdoor picnic areas where you can relax and soak in the beauty of your surroundings while savouring a glass of wine.

Some wineries specialise in organic or biodynamic practices, while others focus on sustainability or rare varietals. You can create an itinerary that suits your preferences and ensures a well-rounded experience. It is worth mentioning that Napa Valley is not just about wine. The region also offers a vibrant culinary scene that perfectly complements its wines.

From Michelin-starred restaurants to charming farm-to-table eateries, there is no shortage of options to satisfy your taste buds. Many wineries have their own restaurants or offer food pairings with their wines, allowing you to indulge in delightful gastronomic experiences.

Exploring Napa Valley's picturesque wineries and experiencing wine-tasting tours is an unforgettable journey for any wine lover. From the breathtaking landscapes to the exceptional wines and culinary delights, this region has it all. Cheers to Napa Valley!

Mendoza, Argentina: Discovering the Charm of South American Wine Culture Amidst the Andes

Located at the foothills of the mighty Andes, Mendoza boasts a unique combination of favourable climate, fertile soil, and passionate winemakers that make it a wine lover's paradise. The region is known for producing some of the world's best Malbec wines, renowned for their rich flavours and velvety textures.

One of the best ways to experience Mendoza's wine culture is by embarking on a wine tour. There are numerous tour operators that offer guided visits to the region's most prestigious wineries, allowing you to explore their vineyards, learn about the winemaking process, and of course, indulge in tastings.

From boutique family-owned wineries to larger estates with centuries-old traditions, each visit offers a unique insight into Mendoza's winemaking heritage. A must-visit destination for wine lovers is the Valle de Uco, located about an hour's drive from Mendoza city. This picturesque valley is home to some of Argentina's most prestigious wineries. Here, you can witness firsthand the meticulous care that goes into producing high-quality wines while enjoying spectacular views of the snow-capped Andes in the background.

If you are interested in learning more about Mendoza's wine culture and history, a visit to the Museo del Vino is a must. This museum showcases the evolution of winemaking in the region and offers guided tours that take you through its fascinating exhibits. You will gain a deeper understanding of how Mendoza became synonymous with exceptional wine production.

Mendoza is not just about wine. The region also offers a plethora of outdoor activities for adventure enthusiasts. From hiking and horseback riding through vineyards to white-water rafting in the Andean rivers, there's no shortage of adrenaline-pumping experiences to complement your wine journey.

When it comes to accommodation, Mendoza offers a range of options to suit every budget and preference. From luxury resorts nestled amidst vineyards to cozy boutique hotels in the heart of the city, you'll find plenty of places to rest and rejuvenate after a day filled with wine tastings and exploration.

Mendoza, Argentina, is a destination that seamlessly blends breathtaking natural beauty with a vibrant wine culture. Whether you're a seasoned wine connoisseur or simply someone who appreciates good wine, Mendoza offers an unforgettable experience that will leave you longing for more.

Chapter 7:

Sustainable Travel: Ethical and Responsible Destinations

Eco-Friendly and Conservation-Oriented Places

Costa Rica: Exploring Sustainable Eco-Lodges and National Parks Dedicated to Conservation

Costa Rica is a paradise for nature enthusiasts and eco-tourists alike. With its breathtaking landscapes, diverse wildlife, and commitment to sustainability, it is no wonder that the country is known for its sustainable eco-lodges and national parks dedicated to conservation.

The country has raised the standard for eco-lodges that are sustainable. These lodges are made to have as little of an impact on the environment as possible while providing guests with cozy and engaging experiences. These eco-lodges go above and above in their dedication to sustainability, utilizing waste management, water conservation, and renewable energy sources.

One such example is Lapa Rios Ecolodge, located on the Osa Peninsula. This lodge is nestled within a private nature reserve and offers guests the opportunity to explore pristine rainforests, spot rare wildlife, and immerse themselves in the local culture. Lapa Rios is not only committed to preserving the environment but also to supporting the local community through various initiatives.

Another notable eco-lodge is Finca Rosa Blanca Coffee Plantation Resort. Situated in the Central Valley, this lodge combines luxury accommodation with sustainable practices. Guests can enjoy organic farm-to-table cuisine, explore the coffee plantation, and relax in beautifully designed rooms that incorporate local materials and traditional craftsmanship.

When it comes to national parks dedicated to conservation, Costa Rica is a shining example. The country boasts an impressive network of protected areas that cover over a quarter of its total land area. These parks are home to a wide variety of ecosystems, including rainforests, cloud forests, wetlands, and marine habitats.

Manuel Antonio National Park is among Costa Rica's most well-known national parks. This park, located on the Pacific coast, is well-known for its breathtaking beaches, verdant jungle, and diverse array of wildlife. Visitors can hike through the park's trails, swim in crystal-clear waters, and spot monkeys, sloths, and colourful birds along the way.

Another must-visit park is Tortuguero National Park on the Caribbean coast. This park is a haven for sea turtles, particularly during nesting season. Visitors can witness the incredible sight of turtles laying their eggs on the beach or watch as baby turtles make their way to the ocean. In addition to turtles, Tortuguero is also home to a rich diversity of flora and fauna, including jaguars, manatees, and countless bird species.

Costa Rica offers a unique opportunity to explore sustainable eco-lodges and national parks dedicated to conservation. Whether you are looking for an immersive experience in nature or simply want to relax in a beautiful setting while knowing you are supporting a worthy cause, Costa Rica has it all. Get ready for an unforgettable journey through this eco-paradise!

Bhutan: Experiencing the World's Only Carbon-Negative Country, Prioritizing Environmental Preservation

Bhutan is a land nestled in the heart of the Himalayas, known for its breathtaking landscapes, rich cultural heritage, and, most notably, its commitment to being the world's only carbon-negative country.

If you are a nature enthusiast or an eco-conscious traveller, Bhutan should definitely be on your bucket list.

So, what exactly does it mean to be carbon-negative? In simple terms, it means that Bhutan absorbs more carbon dioxide from the atmosphere than it emits. This is achieved through a combination of sustainable development practices and a deep-rooted respect for nature.

Bhutan has consciously limited tourism to protect its fragile ecosystems and preserve its cultural authenticity. To visit Bhutan, you must book your trip through a licensed tour operator and pay a daily fee that covers accommodation, meals, transportation, and a sustainable tourism royalty. This approach helps control the number of visitors and ensures that tourism benefits local communities directly.

Once in Bhutan, there are plenty of opportunities to immerse yourself in its awe-inspiring natural beauty. From trekking through pristine forests and exploring ancient monasteries perched atop mountains to spotting rare wildlife and witnessing vibrant traditional festivals, every moment in Bhutan is an experience like no other.

In summary, Bhutan stands as a shining example of what can be achieved when a nation prioritises environmental preservation and sustainable development. Its carbon-negative status, commitment to renewable energy, and unique development philosophy make it a must-visit destination for anyone passionate about protecting our planet. So go ahead and embrace the serenity of the Himalayas, and let Bhutan's natural wonders leave an indelible mark on your soul.

Communities Promoting Sustainable Tourism

Cinque Terre, Italy: Encouraging Responsible Tourism and Preserving Cultural Heritage

Cinque Terre, Italy, is a picturesque and enchanting destination that should be on every traveller's bucket list. Situated along the rugged coastline of the Italian Riviera, this collection of five colourful fishing villages offers breathtaking views, incredible hiking trails, and a laid-back atmosphere that will make you feel like you've stepped back in time.

The five villages that make up Cinque Terre are Monterosso al Mare, Vernazza, Corniglia, Manarola, and Riomaggiore. Each village has its own unique charm and character, but they all share a common thread of beauty and authenticity. From the colourful houses perched on the cliffs to the charming waterfront promenades, there is no shortage of picture-perfect moments in Cinque Terre.

One of the best ways to explore Cinque Terre is by hiking along the famous Sentiero Azzurro, or Blue Trail. This trail connects all five villages and offers stunning views of the coastline. The hike can be challenging at times, but the reward is well worth it. Along the way, you will pass through vineyards, olive groves, and terraced gardens that have been carefully cultivated for centuries.

If hiking is not your thing, there are other activities to keep you entertained in Cinque Terre. The villages are known for their fresh seafood, so be sure to indulge in a delicious seafood meal at one of the local restaurants. You can also spend your days lounging on the beach, exploring the narrow streets and alleyways of the villages, or taking a boat tour along the coast.

Another highlight of Cinque Terre is its vibrant culture and sense of community. Despite being a popular tourist destination, the villages have managed to maintain their authentic charm and local traditions. You will often find locals gathering in the piazzas to chat with friends or enjoy a glass of wine.

In terms of accommodations, there are plenty of options to choose from in Cinque Terre. You can stay in one of the small hotels or bed and breakfasts in the villages themselves or opt for a more secluded option in the surrounding countryside. No matter where you choose to stay, you will be treated to stunning views and a warm Italian welcome.

Cinque Terre is a must-visit destination for anyone who appreciates natural beauty, hiking adventures, delicious food, and a sense of community. Whether you are looking to relax on the beach, explore charming villages, or embark on epic hikes, Cinque Terre has something for everyone.

Grootberg Conservancy, Namibia: Engaging With Local Communities in Sustainable Tourism Initiatives

Grootberg Conservancy in Namibia is a hidden gem worth exploring for any nature lover or adventure seeker. Located in the Kunene region, this Conservancy is known for its breathtaking landscapes, diverse wildlife, and rich cultural heritage.

One of the main attractions of Grootberg Conservancy is its stunning scenery. The Conservancy is nestled between the Etendeka Plateau and the Hoanib River, offering visitors a unique and picturesque landscape to explore. From rugged mountains to deep canyons, this region is a visual treat for anyone who loves the great outdoors.

Grootberg Conservancy is home to an impressive array of wildlife species. Here, you can spot elephants, giraffes, zebras, lions, and even the elusive black rhino. The Conservancy's commitment to conservation has made it a sanctuary for these incredible creatures, providing them with a safe haven to thrive and roam freely. For those interested in immersing themselves in local culture, Grootberg Conservancy offers a chance to interact with the Himba people.

The Himba are a semi-nomadic tribe known for their traditional way of life. Visitors can learn about their customs and traditions and even participate in cultural activities such as traditional dances and craft-making. If you are up for some adventure, Grootberg Conservancy has plenty to offer.

There are numerous hiking trails that take you through the stunning landscapes, allowing you to soak in the beauty of this untouched wilderness. For the more adventurous souls, there are also opportunities for guided multi-day hikes, where you can camp under the starry African sky.

Accommodation options at Grootberg Conservancy are designed to provide visitors with an authentic experience while also ensuring their comfort. From luxurious lodges to eco-friendly campsites, there's something for every type of traveller.

In terms of logistics, Grootberg Conservancy is easily accessible by road. It is located approximately 120 kilometres northwest of Kamanjab, a small town in Namibia. The Conservancy can be reached by a 4x4 vehicle or through organised tours that operate in the area.

Overall, Grootberg Conservancy offers a unique and unforgettable experience for nature enthusiasts. If you want to disconnect from the chaos of everyday life, this Conservancy is your go-to destination.

Kerala, India: Embracing Community-Based Tourism and Supporting Local Economies

Kerala, India, is a beautiful coastal state located in the southwestern part of India. Due to its calm backwaters, abundant vegetation, and lively culture, Kerala has grown in popularity as a travel destination for both domestic and foreign visitors.

Kerala's backwaters, a 900-kilometer system of interconnecting canals, rivers, and lakes, are among its top attractions. Tourists can enjoy a unique and peaceful experience in these backwaters by cruising around the gorgeous scenery aboard traditional houseboats known as "kettuvallams."

The backwaters also provide livelihood to many locals who rely on fishing and farming in these waters. In addition to the backwaters, Kerala is also known for its pristine beaches. With its long coastline along the Arabian Sea, the state offers numerous beach destinations such as Kovalam, Varkala, and Marari. These beaches are perfect for sunbathing, swimming, and indulging in water sports activities.

Kerala's natural beauty extends beyond its waterways and beaches.

Numerous national parks and wildlife sanctuaries that highlight the state's abundant biodiversity may be found there. Thekkady's Periyar National Park is well-known for its elephant herds and tiger reserve. Another place that nature lovers simply must see is the Nilgiri Hills' Silent Valley National Park.

Apart from its natural wonders, Kerala boasts a rich cultural heritage. The state is known for its classical dance forms like Kathakali and Mohiniyattam, which display exquisite costumes and expressive storytelling. Traditional art forms like Theyyam and Kerala mural paintings are also integral to the state's cultural fabric.

When it comes to food, Kerala offers a delectable culinary experience. Known as the land of spices, the state's cuisine is infused with flavours like cardamom, black pepper, cinnamon, and turmeric. Traditional dishes like appam with stew, puttu with kadala curry, and karimeen pollichathu (pearl spot fish) are sure to tantalise your taste buds.

In terms of tourism infrastructure, Kerala has a wide range of accommodation options to suit every budget. From luxury resorts and boutique hotels to budget homestays and guesthouses, there is something for everyone. The hospitality of the locals adds an extra charm to your stay in Kerala.

Kerala is a breathtaking destination that offers a blend of natural beauty, cultural richness, and warm hospitality. Whether you are seeking relaxation amidst serene backwaters or adventure in wildlife sanctuaries, Kerala is the perfect destination. Go ahead and immerse yourself in the enchanting beauty of "God's Own Country".

Supporting Indigenous and Local Initiatives

Taos Pueblo, New Mexico, USA: Immersing in Native American Culture and Supporting Indigenous Communities

Taos Pueblo in New Mexico is a remarkable place that offers a unique opportunity to immerse yourself in Native American culture. Situated at the base of the Sangre de Cristo Mountains, this historic Pueblo has been continuously inhabited for over a thousand years, making it one of the oldest continuously inhabited communities in the United States.

When you visit Taos Pueblo, you'll have the chance to witness firsthand the rich traditions, customs, and way of life of the Taos people. The Pueblo consists of multi-story adobe buildings that have been meticulously preserved, giving you a glimpse into the past and allowing you to appreciate the architectural beauty of this ancient settlement.

One of the highlights of a visit to Taos Pueblo is the opportunity to meet and interact with the local community. The Taos people are known for their warm hospitality and are often willing to share their knowledge and stories with visitors. You can engage in conversations with community members, learn about their history, and gain valuable insights into their culture.

The Pueblo also hosts various cultural events throughout the year, providing visitors with a chance to experience traditional dances, music performances, and other artistic expressions. These events offer a deeper understanding of the spiritual and cultural practices that have shaped the Taos people's way of life.

For those interested in arts and crafts, Taos Pueblo is renowned for its talented artisans who create beautiful handmade pottery, jewellery, and other traditional crafts. You can watch skilled craftsmen at work, learn about their techniques, and even purchase authentic Native American art as a memento of your visit. Nature enthusiasts will also find plenty to explore around Taos Pueblo.

The nearby mountains offer breathtaking hiking trails and opportunities for outdoor activities like fishing and skiing. The landscape surrounding the Pueblo is not only visually stunning but also holds great significance to the Taos people, who consider it sacred.

In terms of logistics, Taos Pueblo is easily accessible from major cities like Santa Fe and Albuquerque. It is important to note that while photography is allowed in certain areas, there are some restrictions out of respect for the cultural sensitivities of the community. It is always best to check with the local authorities or community members before taking any photographs.

A visit to Taos Pueblo is an incredible opportunity to immerse yourself in Native American culture. From exploring the ancient adobe structures to engaging with the local community and witnessing traditional dances and crafts, every aspect of your visit will be a rich and educational experience.

Maasai Mara, Kenya: Participating in Community-Based Tourism Supporting Maasai Tribes

Maasai Mara, Kenya: Community-Based Tourism If you're an adventure seeker and a lover of cultural experiences, then Maasai Mara in Kenya should be at the top of your travel bucket list. Not only is this destination home to breathtaking wildlife and stunning landscapes, but it also offers a unique opportunity to engage in community-based tourism.

Community-based tourism, also known as CBT, is a concept that focuses on empowering local communities by involving them in the tourism industry. It is a win-win situation where travellers get to immerse themselves in the local culture and contribute to the economic development of the community.

In Maasai Mara, the Maasai people are the guardians of this land. They have a deep connection with nature and a rich cultural heritage that has been passed down through generations. By participating in community-based tourism, you not only get to witness their way of life but also actively support their sustainable development.

One popular way to engage with the Maasai community is by staying in a traditional Maasai village, also known as a Manyatta. These villages are designed to provide tourists with an authentic experience while respecting the cultural norms and values of the Maasai people. You can learn about their traditional practices, participate in daily activities such as milking cows or building huts, and even join in on their traditional dances and ceremonies.

Apart from the Manyattas, there are also various community-led initiatives that offer unique experiences. For example, you can go on a guided nature walk with a Maasai warrior who will share his knowledge about the local flora and fauna. You can also visit a local Maasai market where you can buy handmade crafts directly from the artisans themselves.

Engaging in community-based tourism not only provides you with an enriching experience but also has a positive impact on the local community. By supporting local businesses and initiatives, you contribute to the economic growth of the Maasai people, helping them preserve their culture and way of life for future generations.

In addition to the cultural aspect, Maasai Mara is also famous for its incredible wildlife. The Maasai Mara National Reserve is home to an abundance of wildlife, including lions, elephants, giraffes, zebras, and wildebeests. Taking a safari through the reserve is an absolute must-do activity while visiting this region.

When planning your trip to Maasai Mara, it is essential to choose tour operators or accommodations that actively support community-based tourism initiatives. Look for organisations that have partnerships with local communities and prioritise sustainable practices. This way, you can ensure that your visit has a positive impact on both the environment and the local people.

Immersion in the rich culture of the Maasai people and community-based tourism are two exceptional opportunities that Maasai Mara provides. In addition to making lifelong memories, you can help the local community thrive sustainably by getting involved in activities that directly benefit and include them.

Ait Benhaddou, Morocco: Engaging With Local Artisans and Supporting Traditional Craftsmanship

Ait Benhaddou, Morocco, is a hidden gem that supports traditional craftsmanship in the most enchanting way.

This UNESCO World Heritage Site, which is tucked away in the foothills of the Atlas Mountains, is not only a breathtaking example of Moroccan architecture but also a living demonstration of the extraordinary skills and craftsmanship that have been passed down through the years.

When you visit Ait Benhaddou, you will be transported back in time as you wander through its narrow alleys and marvel at the intricate details of the earthen buildings. The entire village is made entirely of mud and straw, and the walls are adorned with beautiful geometric patterns and motifs.

One of the most fascinating aspects of Ait Benhaddou is its thriving artisanal community. Here, you can witness traditional craftsmen at work, honing their skills and creating masterpieces that are truly awe-inspiring. From intricate metalwork to vibrant textiles, every piece is a testament to the rich cultural heritage of this region.

Ait Benhaddou is also known for his carpet weaving. The women of the village spend countless hours meticulously hand-weaving these beautiful rugs, using techniques that have been passed down for centuries. Each rug tells a story, with vibrant colours and intricate patterns that are unique to each weaver.

Another craft that thrives in Ait Benhaddou is pottery. The potters here create stunning earthenware using traditional techniques that have been perfected over generations. From delicate vases to functional cooking pots, every piece is a work of art that showcases the skill and creativity of the craftsmen. But it is not just about the crafts themselves; it is also about the preservation of these traditional skills.

Ait Benhaddou recognises the importance of supporting and promoting traditional craftsmanship, not just for its economic value but also to ensure that these skills are not lost to time. The village has established workshops and training programs to pass on these skills to the younger generation. By doing so, they are not only preserving their cultural heritage but also providing opportunities for local artisans to earn a living from their craft.

In addition to supporting traditional craftsmanship, Ait Benhaddou also serves as a hub for cultural exchange. The village attracts visitors from all over the world who come to appreciate the beauty of its architecture and crafts. This interaction between locals and tourists fosters understanding and appreciation for different cultures, creating a more interconnected global community.

So, if you are looking for an authentic experience that celebrates traditional craftsmanship, Ait Benhaddou should be at the top of your travel bucket list. Immerse yourself in the rich history and culture of this remarkable village, and witness firsthand the incredible skills of its craftsmen. The experience will be unforgettable.

Chapter 8:

Adventure and Exploration

Trekking and Hiking Expeditions

The Appalachian Trail, USA: Embarking on a Long-Distance Hiking Experience Through Diverse Landscapes

Embarking on a long-distance hiking experience through the Appalachian Trail in the USA is an adventure like no other. Spanning over 2,000 miles, the Appalachian Trail offers hikers a chance to immerse themselves in the beauty and diversity of the American landscape. From lush forests to breathtaking mountain peaks, this trail is a true treasure for nature enthusiasts.

From Springer Mountain in Georgia to Mount Katahdin in Maine, the Appalachian Trail, sometimes known as the AT, runs for a distance. The fourteen states it travels through include Virginia, West Virginia, North Carolina, Georgia, Pennsylvania, New Jersey, New York, Connecticut, Massachusetts, Vermont, New Hampshire, and Maine.

Each state offers its own unique scenery and challenges, making the AT a truly unforgettable experience. One of the most remarkable aspects of the Appalachian Trail is its diverse landscape. Hikers will encounter everything from dense forests and rolling meadows to rocky ridges and breathtaking waterfalls.

Along with many other beautiful places, the trail passes through the White Mountains, Shenandoah National Park, and the Great Smoky Mountains National Park. Along the way, hikers are inspired and energized by the constantly changing surroundings. A long-distance journey such as the Appalachian Trail demands meticulous planning and preparation before beginning.

It is essential to have proper gear and equipment, including a sturdy backpack, comfortable hiking boots, and lightweight camping gear. It is also important to have a well-thought-out itinerary that takes into account your physical abilities and time constraints. While hiking the AT can be physically demanding, it is also an incredibly rewarding experience. The sense of accomplishment that comes with completing such a challenging journey is unparalleled.

Along the way, hikers will have the opportunity to meet fellow adventurers from all walks of life. The trail community is known for its camaraderie and supportiveness, creating a unique sense of belonging. In terms of logistics, there are several options for resupplying food and obtaining water along the trail. Many hikers choose to send resupply boxes to post offices or hostels along the way, while others rely on grocery stores and restaurants located near the trail.

Water sources are abundant throughout most of the trail, but it is important to carry a water filter or purification system to ensure safe drinking water. It is worth noting that hiking the entire Appalachian Trail can take several months to complete.

Most thru-hikers start their journey in early spring or late winter to maximise their chances of completing the trail before winter weather sets in. However, many hikers choose to section hike the trail, completing it in smaller portions over a longer period of time.

Before embarking on this epic adventure, it is crucial to familiarise yourself with Leave No Trace principles. These guidelines help minimise your impact on the environment and preserve the beauty of the trail for future generations. Respecting wildlife, properly disposing of waste, and staying on designated trails are just a few examples of how you can practice Leave No Trace ethics.

Embarking on a long-distance hiking experience through the Appalachian Trail in the USA is an incredible adventure that showcases the diverse beauty of America's landscape. The trail offers hikers an opportunity to challenge themselves physically while immersing themselves in nature's wonders. With proper planning and preparation, you can create memories that will last a lifetime on this iconic trail.

The Camino de Santiago, Spain: Walking the Historic Pilgrimage Route and Experiencing Diverse Cultures

The Camino is not just about the physical challenge of walking long distances, it is also about immersing yourself in the rich culture and history of Spain. A network of paths called the Camino de Santiago, or the Way of St. James, guides travellers to the shrine of the apostle St. James the Great, located in the Santiago de Compostela Cathedral.

While there are many routes to choose from, the most popular one is the Camino Francés, which starts in St. Jean Pied de Port on the French side of the Pyrenees and ends in Santiago de Compostela. One of the most remarkable things about walking the Camino is the sense of community and camaraderie that you will experience along the way.

Pilgrims from all walks of life come together to share stories, support each other, and forge lasting friendships. It is a truly unique and uplifting experience. In addition to the social aspect, the Camino also offers a diverse cultural experience. As you walk through different regions of Spain, you will encounter a wide range of landscapes, architecture, and cuisine.

From the lush green valleys of Galicia to the rugged mountains of Leon and the vineyards of La Rioja, every day brings something new and exciting. The Camino is not just for religious pilgrims. Many people undertake this journey for personal reasons – to find spiritual enlightenment, to challenge themselves physically and mentally, or simply to take a break from their everyday lives.

While walking the Camino can be physically demanding, it is important to remember that it's not a race. Take your time, listen to your body, and enjoy the journey. There are plenty of accommodations along the way, ranging from albergues (pilgrim hostels) to hotels, so you can choose what suits your comfort level.

In terms of logistics, there are several ways to approach the Camino. Some people choose to walk the entire route in one go, which usually takes around 30-35 days. Others break it up into smaller sections and come back year after year to complete it. There is no right or wrong way to do it – it's all about what works best for you.

Walking the Camino de Santiago is a truly remarkable experience that offers a unique blend of physical challenge, cultural immersion, and personal growth. Whether you are seeking spiritual enlightenment or simply want to embark on an unforgettable adventure, the Camino is the best destination. Get ready to embark on a journey that will stay with you long after you have reached Santiago de Compostela. Buen Camino!

Extreme Sports and Thrilling Adventures

Interlaken, Switzerland: Paragliding Over the Swiss Alps and Exploring Adventure Sports

Interlaken, Switzerland, is a dream destination for adventure enthusiasts and adrenaline junkies alike. This picturesque town, nestled between two stunning lakes, Lake Brienz and Lake Thun, offers a plethora of thrilling activities that will leave you breathless and wanting more.

One of the most popular adventure sports in Interlaken is paragliding. Paragliding in Interlaken is an experience like no other, and it is guaranteed to get your heart racing. If you're new to paragliding, there are plenty of professional instructors and tandem pilots who will guide you through this exhilarating activity. They will teach you the basics of paragliding, ensure your safety throughout the flight, and even capture stunning photos and videos for you to cherish as lifelong memories.

Paragliding in Interlaken is not just about the adrenaline rush; it also involves taking in the breathtaking scenery that is all around you. Enjoy expansive vistas of the Eiger, Mönch, and Jungfrau mountains—three famous peaks that dominate the Swiss Alps landscape—as you soar into the skies.

Apart from paragliding, Interlaken offers a wide range of other adventure sports for thrill-seekers.

If you enjoy being in the water, you can try your hand at river rafting or canyoning on the Aare River. Canyoning is a sport that includes swimming in natural pools, rappelling down waterfalls, and winding through slender canyons. It is an action-packed activity that will push your limits and give you an adrenaline rush like no other.

For those who prefer to stay on solid ground, bungee jumping is another popular adventure sport in Interlaken. Leap off a platform suspended high above a stunning valley and feel the rush of freefall before being brought back up by the bungee cord. It is an experience that will make your heart race and leave you craving for more.

If you are looking for something slightly tamer but still thrilling, consider taking a helicopter ride over the Swiss Alps. Marvel at the majestic mountains from a bird's eye view and snap some envy-inducing photos to share with your friends and family.

Interlaken truly is a haven for adventure sports enthusiasts. Go to the Swiss town and immerse yourself in an incredible adventure! It does not matter if you are an experienced adrenaline addict or someone eager to try something different and step beyond their comfort zone; you will enjoy your trip!

Moab, Utah, USA: Rock Climbing, Mountain Biking, and Exploring the Rugged Terrain of Red Rock Country

Moab is renowned for its world-class climbing routes that attract climbers from all over the globe. The sandstone cliffs and towers provide a unique challenge and breathtaking views. One of the most famous climbing areas is Indian Creek, known for its iconic crack climbing. The splitter cracks offer a variety of challenges for both beginners and experienced climbers.

If mountain biking is more your style, you are in for a treat. Moab boasts some of the best mountain biking trails in the world. The famous Slickrock Trail is a must-ride for any serious mountain biker. The slick rock surface provides unmatched traction and an exhilarating ride.

Other popular trails include Porcupine Rim, Amasa Back, and the Whole Enchilada. These trails offer a mix of technical sections, stunning scenery, and adrenaline-pumping descents. But it is not just about rock climbing and mountain biking in Moab. The rugged terrain begs to be explored by foot as well.

Take a hike through Arches National Park and witness the iconic Delicate Arch up close. The park offers numerous trails of varying difficulty levels, allowing you to immerse yourself in the natural beauty of the red rocks. Canyonlands National Park is another gem that should not be missed. Its vast canyons and towering mesas provide endless opportunities for exploration.

When you are done with your outdoor adventures, Moab itself is a charming town with a vibrant atmosphere. You will find a range of accommodation options, from luxurious resorts to cozy campgrounds catering to all budgets. The town also offers a variety of dining options to satisfy your post-adventure cravings.

Do not forget to check out the local shops and art galleries for unique souvenirs. As with any adventure destination, safety should be a top priority. Make sure to come prepared with appropriate gear, check the weather conditions, and always follow local regulations and guidelines. It is also worth considering hiring a guide or joining a tour if you are not familiar with the area.

Moab, Utah, is a paradise for outdoor enthusiasts seeking thrilling experiences in a stunning natural setting. Whether you are an avid rock climber, mountain biker, or simply enjoy exploring rugged terrain, Moab has it all. Get ready for an unforgettable journey in Red Rock country!

Wildlife Expeditions and Conservation Volunteering

Orangutan Conservation Projects, Borneo: Volunteering in Rehabilitation Centres and Aiding Orangutan Conservation Efforts

Volunteering in Borneo to contribute to the Orangutan Conservation Projects is an experience that will not only change your life but also make a significant impact on the conservation efforts of these incredible creatures. Borneo, the third-largest island in the world, is home to over 50,000 orangutans, making it a crucial destination for anyone passionate about wildlife conservation.

Why should you choose Borneo for your volunteering journey? Here are the reasons:

1. Conservation Efforts: Orangutans are critically endangered due to deforestation, illegal pet trade, and habitat loss. By volunteering in Borneo, you become part of a community dedicated to protecting these magnificent primates. Your contribution will involve activities such as habitat restoration, wildlife monitoring, and educating local communities about sustainable practices.

2. Immersive Experience: Travelling to Borneo offers a unique opportunity to witness

orangutans in their natural habitat. You will have the chance to observe their behaviour, learn about their social structures, and gain a deeper understanding of their plight. This immersive experience will undoubtedly create lifelong memories and a passion for wildlife conservation.

3. Cultural Exchange: Besides working with orangutans, volunteering in Borneo allows you to immerse yourself in the rich culture of the local communities. Interacting with indigenous tribes, such as the Iban and Dayak people, will open your eyes to their way of life, traditions, and long-standing connection with nature. This cultural exchange adds another layer of depth to your volunteering journey.

4. Personal Growth: Volunteering abroad is not just about helping others; it is also an opportunity for personal growth. Working in challenging environments with limited resources fosters resilience, adaptability, and problem-solving skills. You will develop a greater sense of empathy and appreciation for our planet's biodiversity, inspiring you to make sustainable choices even after your volunteering experience ends.

5. Networking and Future Opportunities: Volunteering in Borneo connects you with like-minded individuals from around the world who share your passion for conservation. Building relationships with fellow volunteers, researchers, and local experts can open doors

to future opportunities within the field of wildlife conservation or environmental advocacy.

Before embarking on your journey, it is essential to do thorough research and choose a reputable organisation or project that aligns with your values and goals. Look for projects that prioritise animal welfare, have a strong track record of community engagement, and provide necessary support and training for volunteers.

Volunteering is not a one-time solution but a small piece of a larger puzzle in protecting orangutans and their habitat. Your efforts contribute to long-term conservation strategies that aim to create sustainable solutions for both wildlife and local communities.

Travelling to Borneo to volunteer in the Orangutan Conservation Projects is an incredible opportunity to make a tangible difference in the lives of orangutans while immersing yourself in a vibrant culture. By joining forces with dedicated individuals who share your passion, you can contribute to preserving one of our planet's most precious species for generations to come. Embrace this once-in-a-lifetime adventure, and be part of something extraordinary!

The Amazon Rainforest, Brazil: Participating in Wildlife Conservation and Research Programmes in the World's Largest Rainforest

Travelling to the Amazon Rainforest in Brazil to participate in wildlife conservation sounds is an amazing adventure. Not only will you get to experience one of the most biodiverse regions on the planet, but you will also be making a positive impact on the preservation of its unique and fragile ecosystem.

Firstly, it is important to understand the significance of the Amazon Rainforest. It is sometimes referred to as the "lungs of the Earth" because of its ability to produce oxygen and control the climate. It is located in nine South American countries, including Brazil. Moreover, the Amazon is home to a staggering variety of endemic—found nowhere else in the world—plant and animal species.

To participate in wildlife conservation in the Amazon, there are several organisations and initiatives that offer volunteer programs. These programs typically focus on various aspects of conservation, such as researching endangered species, monitoring biodiversity, habitat restoration, and community education.

One renowned organisation in Brazil is Instituto Mamirauá, located in the heart of the Amazon. They offer volunteer opportunities where you can assist with their ongoing research projects, such as studying river dolphins or monitoring jaguars. These projects not only contribute to scientific knowledge but also help inform conservation efforts.

Another prominent organisation is the Amazon Environmental Research Institute (IPAM). They work on a wide range of conservation projects, including sustainable agriculture, forest management, and indigenous rights. By joining their volunteer program, you can actively contribute to their initiatives and gain valuable insights into the challenges faced by local communities.

When planning your trip, it is essential to consider the logistics and safety aspects. The Amazon Rainforest is a vast and remote area with specific requirements for travel and accommodation. It is strongly recommended to work with a reputable tour operator or organisation that specialises in eco-tourism and conservation.

Prior to embarking on your journey, it is advisable to do some research on the flora and fauna of the Amazon Rainforest. Understanding the unique ecosystem and its inhabitants will not only enhance your experience but also enable you to better contribute to wildlife conservation efforts.

Travelling to the Amazon Rainforest in Brazil for wildlife conservation is an incredible opportunity to immerse yourself in nature while making a difference. By joining volunteer programs or working with reputable organisations, you can actively contribute to preserving this invaluable ecosystem.

Conclusion

The book, *50 Places to Visit Before You Die*, is undoubtedly a moment of reflection and inspiration. Throughout this book, we have delved into some of the world's most awe-inspiring locations, from the bustling streets of New York City to the exquisite beauty of the Taj Mahal.

Each place has its own unique charm and allure, leaving an indelible mark on those who have had the privilege of experiencing it. One cannot discuss bucket list destinations without mentioning the majestic wonder that is Machu Picchu. Nestled high in the Andes Mountains of Peru, this ancient Incan city never fails to captivate visitors with its breathtaking views and fascinating history. Standing atop Huayna Picchu and taking in the panoramic vistas is a moment that will stay with you forever.

No bucket list would be complete without a visit to the iconic city of Paris. The Eiffel Tower, Louvre Museum, and Notre Dame Cathedral are just a few of the landmarks that have made Paris an eternal symbol of romance and elegance. Exploring the charming streets and indulging in delectable pastries at local patisseries is an experience that will make you fall in love with this city time and time again.

As we conclude our journey through these 50 remarkable destinations, it is important to remember that a bucket list is not just about ticking off places; it is about embracing new experiences, broadening our horizons, and creating lifelong memories.

Whether you have checked off all 50 places or have only just begun your journey, may this book serve as a reminder to live life to the fullest and seize every opportunity to explore this beautiful world we live in. Let it inspire you to keep adding new destinations to your own personal bucket list and continue embracing the wonders that await.

References

About Masai Mara & conservancies. (n.d.). Masai Mara. https://www.masaimara.com/information-masai-mara.php

Anse Source d'Argent. (n.d.). Lonley Plant. https://www.lonelyplanet.com/seychelles/la-digue/attractions/anse-source-d-argent/a/poi-sig/1402802/355594

Connell, T. J., and Rodriguez, V. (2024, January 7). Barcelona. In *Encyclopedia Britannica.* Retrieved January 8, 2024. https://www.britannica.com/place/Barcelona

Coodley, L. (2023, December 22). Napa. In *Encyclopedia Britannica.* Retrieved January 8, 2024. https://www.britannica.com/place/Napa

Encyclopedia Britannica. (n.d.-1). Antarctica summary. In *Encyclopedia Britannica.* Retrieved January 8, 2024. https://www.britannica.com/summary/Antarctica

Encyclopedia Britannica. (n.d.-2). *Appalachian national scenic trail.* In *Encyclopedia Britannica.* https://www.britannica.com/place/Appalachian-National-Scenic-Trail

Encyclopedia Britannica. (n.d.-3). *Belize barrier reef*. In *Encyclopedia Britannica*. Retrieved January 8, 2024. https://www.britannica.com/place/Belize-Barrier-Reef

Encyclopedia Britannica. (n.d.-4). Bordeaux. In *Encyclopedia Britannica*. Retrieved January 8, 2024. https://www.britannica.com/place/Bordeaux

Encyclopedia Britannica. (n.d.-5). Borneo. In *Encyclopedia Britannica*. Retrieved January 8, 2024. https://www.britannica.com/place/Borneo-island-Pacific-Ocean

Encyclopedia Britannica. (n.d.-6). Cappadocia. In *Encyclopedia Britannica*. Retrieved January 8, 2024. https://www.britannica.com/place/Cappadocia

Encyclopedia Britannica. (n.d.-7). Colorado Plateau. In *Encyclopedia Britannica*. Retrieved January 8, 2024. https://www.britannica.com/place/Colorado-Plateau

Encyclopedia Britannica. (n.d.-8). Fès. In *Encyclopedia Britannica*. Retrieved January 8, 2024. https://www.britannica.com/place/Fes

Encyclopedia Britannica. (n.d.-9). Galapagos Islands. In *Encyclopedia Britannica*. Retrieved January 8, 2024. https://www.britannica.com/place/Galapagos-Islands

Encyclopedia Britannica. (n.d.-10). Grand Canyon. In *Encyclopedia Britannica*. Retrieved January 8, 2024.

https://www.britannica.com/place/Grand-Canyon

Encyclopedia Britannica. (n.d.-11). Great Barrier Reef. In *Encyclopedia Britannica*. Retrieved January 8, 2024. https://www.britannica.com/place/Great-Barrier-Reef

Encyclopedia Britannica. (n.d.-12). Interlaken. In *Encyclopedia Britannica*. Retrieved January 8, 2024. https://www.britannica.com/place/Interlaken

Encyclopedia Britannica. (n.d.-13). Kilimanjaro. In *Encyclopedia Britannica*. Retrieved January 8, 2024. https://www.britannica.com/place/Kilimanjaro

Encyclopedia Britannica. (n.d.-14). La Spezia. In *Encyclopedia Britannica*. Retrieved January 8, 2024. https://www.britannica.com/place/La-Spezia-Italy

Encyclopedia Britannica. (n.d.-15). Machu Picchu. In *Encyclopedia Britannica*. Retrieved January 8, 2024. https://www.britannica.com/place/Machu-Picchu

Encyclopedia Britannica. (n.d.-16). Marrakech. In *Encyclopedia Britannica*. Retrieved January 8, 2024. https://www.britannica.com/place/Marrakech

Encyclopedia Britannica. (n.d.-17). Mendoza. In *Encyclopedia Britannica*. Retrieved January 8, 2024.

https://www.britannica.com/place/Mendoza-Argentina

Encyclopedia Britannica. (n.d.-18). Oaxaca. In *Encyclopedia Britannica*. Retrieved January 8, 2024. https://www.britannica.com/place/Oaxaca-state-Mexico

Encyclopedia Britannica. (n.d.-19). Petra. In *Encyclopedia Britannica*. Retrieved January 8, 2024. https://www.britannica.com/place/Petra-ancient-city-Jordan

Encyclopedia Britannica. (n.d.-20). *Santiago de Compostela*. In *Encyclopedia Britannica*. Retrieved January 8, 2024. https://www.britannica.com/place/Santiago-de-Compostela

Encyclopedia Britannica. (n.d.-21). Serengeti National Park. In *Encyclopedia Britannica*. Retrieved January 8, 2024. https://www.britannica.com/place/Serengeti-National-Park

Encyclopedia Britannica. (n.d.-22). Sawai Madhopur. In *Encyclopedia Britannica*. Retrieved January 8, 2024. https://www.britannica.com/place/Sawai-Madhopur

Encyclopedia Britannica. (n.d.-23). Socotra. In *Encyclopedia Britannica*. Retrieved January 8, 2024. https://www.britannica.com/place/Socotra

Encyclopedia Britannica. (n.d.-24). Svalbard. In *Encyclopedia Britannica*. Retrieved January 8, 2024. https://www.britannica.com/place/Svalbard

Encyclopedia Britannica. (n.d.-25). Taj Mahal. In *Encyclopedia Britannica*. Retrieved January 8, 2024. https://www.britannica.com/topic/Taj-Mahal

Encyclopedia Britannica. (n.d.-26). Taos. In *Encyclopedia Britannica*. Retrieved January 8, 2024. https://www.britannica.com/place/Taos-New-Mexico

Encyclopedia Britannica. (n.d.-27). Tokyo. In *Encyclopedia Britannica*. Retrieved January 8, 2024. https://www.britannica.com/place/Tokyo

Encyclopedia Britannica. (n.d.-28). Uyuni Salt Flat. In *Encyclopedia Britannica*. Retrieved January 8, 2024. https://www.britannica.com/place/Uyuni-Salt-Flat

Elbow, G., Stansfier, C. L., & Karnes, T. L. (n.d.). Costa Rica. In *Encyclopedia Britannica*. Retrieved January 8, 2024. https://www.britannica.com/place/Costa-Rica

Enrlich, B., Ardagh, J. A. C., & Daul, K. (n.d.). Paris. In *Encyclopedia Britannica*. Retrieved January 8, 2024. https://www.britannica.com/place/Paris

Gritzner, J. A., & Peel, R. F. (n.d.) Sahara. In *Encyclopedia Britannica*. Retrieved January 8, 2024. https://www.britannica.com/place/Sahara-desert-Africa

Grootberg Lodge. (n.d.). Tripadvisor. https://www.tripadvisor.co.za/Hotel_Review-g13228161-d969656-Reviews-Grootberg_Lodge-Palmwag_Damaraland.html

Grubor. (2014, January 16). *Navagio Beach, Zakinthos, Greece*. Atlas Obscura. https://www.atlasobscura.com/places/navagio-beach

Karan, P. P., & Norbu, D. (n.d.). Bhutan. In *Encyclopedia Britannica*. Retrieved January 8, 2024. https://www.britannica.com/place/Bhutan

Ksar of Ait-Ben-Haddou. (n.d.). UNESCO. https://whc.unesco.org/en/list/444/

Noble, W. A. (n.d.). Kerala. In *Encyclopedia Britannica*. Retrieved January 8, 2024. https://www.britannica.com/place/Kerala

Raja Ampat Islands, Indonesia, Asia. (n.d.). Lonely Planet. https://www.lonelyplanet.com/indonesia/raja-ampat-islands

Sepilok orangutan sanctuary. (n.d.). Natural World Safaris. https://www.naturalworldsafaris.com/asia/borneo/safaris-and-planning/sepilok-orangutan-sanctuary

Torre del Paine national park. (n.d.). Go Chile. https://www.gochile.cl/en/torres-del-paine-national-park/

Tour options. (n.d.). Ocean Dynamics. https://www.oceandynamics.com.au/experienc es

Scudiere, P., & Campbell, A. K. (n.d.). New York. In *Encyclopedia Britannica*. Retrieved January 8, 2024. https://www.britannica.com/place/New-York-state

Sternstein, L. (n.d.). Bangkok. In *Encyclopedia Britannica*. Retrieved January 8, 2024. https://www.britannica.com/place/Bangkok

Venables, S., Hunt, J., & Tenzing, N. (n.d.). Mount Everest. In *Encyclopedia Britannica*. Retrieved January 8, 2024. https://www.britannica.com/place/Mount-Everest

Printed in Poland
by Amazon Fulfillment
Poland Sp. z o.o., Wrocław

30979764R00094